The Power, Passion & Pain of Black Love

Cover and chapter heading illustrations by Reginald Mackey

First edition, fourth printing

Copyright 1993 by Jawanza Kunjufu
(Kiswahili for Dependable and Cheerful)

African American Images
Chicago, Illinois

The

Power,

Passion

&

Pain  of

Black

Love

by Jawanza Kunjufu

TABLE OF CONTENTS

DEDICATION

*This book is lovingly dedicated to my wife,
Rita, who is my very best friend, a loving
and giving companion, my soul mate, and
my number one prayer partner. As a wife,
you're the best and I know I don't deserve
you - I guess this is but another example
of what my Lord calls grace.*

*To my readers, please pass this book on
to our youth, who become sexually active
so early, to those couples who are
married, shacking or engaged, and to those
who are physically and emotionally separated.*

ACKNOWLEDGMENTS

I thank God for the idea and the ability to write this book and for the wonderful way that He continues to work in my marriage. I thank our production staff members for their typing, designing, and editorial assistance. I'm also very grateful to my friend Diane Mayes for coming up with the title for this book. I thank Val and Ethel Jordan for being marital godparents to Rita and I.

Throughout the book, the pronoun "we" will be used in the collective sense to indicate that I am part of a collective and did not write this book alone.

Use the list of anecdotes as a tool to have an open discussion about male/female relationships.

 # Chapter 1

Male/Female Anecdotes

If there is one subject that creates a lot of furor and receives a lot of attention, generalizations and stereotypes, it is the discussion on male/female relationships. There are many stereotypes, generalizations and polemic statements that are disbursed among the community, some true and some false. People seldom qualify the accusations that they make about an entire gender of the population.

Listed below are anecdotes that either I have developed or heard from others. I would like you to read these anecdotes and pause after reading each of them to assess your feelings about them. These are so thought-provoking that you may want to use them in a group for further discussion. As the author, I am not stating that I agree with all of these, but I do think that these anecdotes and many more need to be mentioned and discussed if we are going to improve Black male/female relationships.

When a man is not in his natural place, woman is misplaced, child is displaced, and God is replaced.

♥♥♥♥

Some women give sex for love.

Some men give love for sex.

♥♥♥♥

Women give sex, and men get sex.

♥♥♥♥

When you have sex with a person, you have sex with his/her history.

♥♥♥♥

Which way - vaginal, oral or anal?

♥♥♥♥

Let me hold you tight, if only for one night.

♥♥♥♥

I love you because you make me feel good.

♥♥♥♥

What's love got to do with it?

♥♥♥♥

I want to spend all of my tomorrows with you, and if I can't, I hope tomorrow never comes.

♥♥♥♥

Men want women to stay the same.

♥♥♥♥

Women want men to change (to grow up).

♥♥♥♥

A woman has four options with her man: she can be a partner, mother, toy or parole officer.

♥♥♥♥

Most men are dogs.

♥♥♥♥

Most women want you to spend money on them.

♥♥♥♥

Diamonds are a girl's best friend.

♥♥♥♥

Boys shack; men marry.

Boys want quantity, while men seek quality.

♥♥♥♥

*Once there were pretty women and working men,
now there are pretty men and working women.*

♥♥♥♥

*Black men and women are equal but not identical.
She may be able to work construction, but he can't give
birth and breastfeed children.*

♥♥♥♥

*Little girls grow up dreaming of ways to catch a man.
Little boys grow up dreaming of ways to buy a car.*

♥♥♥♥

*Some Black women respect you when you slap them
around every once in a while.*

♥♥♥♥

*Show me a husband who's not hen-pecked, and I'll
show you a man who is not happy.*

♥♥♥♥

*Can a mama's boy respect his woman if he doesn't
respect his mama?*

♥♥♥♥

*What can a Black man or woman do for me that a
White man or woman can't do better?*

♥♥♥♥

*I don't believe opposites attract at the gut level;
I believe like attracts like. While courting,
you are looking for the evidence.*

♥♥♥♥

*We do a better job choosing our cars, clothes, houses,
colleges and careers than selecting a mate.*

♥♥♥♥

*There is nothing worse than marrying a mama's boy,
or a woman who never had a daddy or
a significant male at home.*

3

Ain't nothing going on; we're just friends.

♥♥♥♥

Men and women can't be friends until they confirm they will not be sexually active with each other.

♥♥♥♥

That's my man/woman, and you better not look at, talk to or put your hands on him/her.

♥♥♥♥

What would it be like being married to me?

♥♥♥♥

We are nicer and more respectful to strangers than we are to our spouses.

♥♥♥♥

We would not have any problems if he/she simply did things my way.

♥♥♥♥

Do you want to be right, or do you want to be married?

♥♥♥♥

I get tired of disagreeing with my spouse if it means I'm going to be correct - but by myself for the evening.

♥♥♥♥

The man is the head of the house, but the woman is the neck; it's the neck that turns the head.

♥♥♥♥

Marriage boils down to diapers, dishes, homework, bills, and a little romance.

♥♥♥♥

I left because he/she didn't make me happy.

♥♥♥♥

When the marriage is bad, it's bad, and when it's good, it's good, but how would I know if I didn't stay?

♥♥♥♥

It's obvious that people want to be married; they try over and over and over again.

Marriage and family are the major reasons for existence.

♥♥♥♥

Most single people want to be married, and many married people want to be single.

♥♥♥♥

I think of a dissolved marriage as yesterday's meal. It was good, but it's over; now it's time to flush.

♥♥♥♥

If the major problem for Africans is White supremacy, then the family must come together to defeat the problem.

♥♥♥♥

In the 1950's, women said, "I will marry a man at any cost, especially to live in a house." In the 1990's, women say, "I can be miserable by myself, in my own apartment or condo."

♥♥♥♥

I don't need a man for money, a car, house or baby. I can get all these by myself.

♥♥♥♥

Why do we have to get married in the White man's court? She knows I love her. Besides, we need to live together and see how this works first.

♥♥♥♥

What's the difference between polygamy and serial monogamy?

♥♥♥♥

I don't deserve you; I'm not good enough for you. I need to find myself.

♥♥♥♥

Do you love your mate as unconditionally as your parents love you?

♥♥♥♥

Whoever is the most committed to the relationship has the least power in it.

In African values, $1+1=1$, while in European values,
$1+0=1$.

♥♥♥♥

Love is a verb, not a noun. Love is sacrificing,
listening, empathizing, appreciating and affirming.

♥♥♥♥

There is nothing wrong with marriage that sacrifice
and compromise can't conquer.

♥♥♥♥

I hope these anecdotes have generated a greater interest in finding out more about male/female relationships. Many of these anecdotes will be discussed throughout the following chapters. Let's now move to the next chapter and take an inside look at what's really going on between Black men and women.

Couples need to address and separate the effect external events and situations have on a relationship.

♥ CHAPTER II

WHAT'S LOVE GOT TO DO WITH IT?

Shared below are some scenarios that many of us have experienced over the years. The issues that are reflected in these scenarios will be analyzed from a macro perspective in the following chapter.

♥♥♥♥

Renee and Jeffery had been married for ten years. It had been a beautiful marriage. Renee often thought about the 368 people who were present at the wedding ceremony. Yet none of the guests were there when she needed them the most. In the eleventh year, things had taken a downward turn. Jeffery just wasn't the same. She knew it started when the GM plant created a lockout three years ago in their fight against the union. The union eventually conceded and was allowed to continue to work, but GM was not satisfied with those concessions and eventually closed the plant. Renee noticed that during the lockout, Jeffery would toss and turn in his sleep and would sometimes wake up in a cold sweat saying, "I need my job." Renee glanced around the beautiful house they had lived in for the past five years. She noticed the elegant dining room set, nice living room furniture, and the plush carpet in the family room. Life had really been good to them. They had been considered the ideal couple. That was when Jeffery was making $18 an hour and working at least ten to twelve hours a day; there were even some months when he was able to work six days a week.

GM eventually decided that it was more productive and cost efficient for them to relocate the plant from their midwest location to Mexico. Renee just couldn't seem to understand how the global economy was putting a damper on her marriage. It was becoming more and more difficult to talk to Jeffery. Renee would come home from work at 5:30 or 6:00, and Jeffery was nowhere to be found. On the days when Jeffery was there or when he did come in before Renee went to sleep, he had very little to say. Renee didn't know what was the most effective approach to deal with Jeffery. Sometimes she would try to assure him that everything was going to be OK because she was working, but as soon as she made that comment, Jeffery would go off and say, "Oh, so you think you can do it without me, huh?" Renee would then say, "No, you don't understand. I didn't mean it like that. I just meant that you've supported us for so long by yourself, and now this is an opportunity for me to return the favor."

Once Jeffery stormed out of the house and didn't come back for three days. Another time he was about ready to slap Renee, and as he held his hand high in the air, Renee shivered because she had never seen Jeffery act like this.

On another occasion, Renee told Jeffery she had heard that they were hiring at a department store. For a long while Jeffery didn't even want to consider working at a department store for $6 an hour. Renee understood that it would be difficult to go from $18 an hour to $6 an hour, but something would be better than nothing says the old adage. Jeffery stayed there for about three months, but one day he "went off" on a customer who wanted a refund for something Jeffery didn't feel was justifiable.

9

Renee knew that wasn't the real reason Jeffery lost the job; she knew her husband was frustrated.

Renee began to cry as she sat drinking a cup of coffee at the kitchen table. Jeffery had moved out several months ago. Renee wrote a letter to Jeffery last week reminding him how it used to be in the good old days when they were dating and didn't have any money. How ironic it was that when they were poor, they were so happy. While it was great to have had these ten years together and to have lived in a beautiful house, Renee told Jeffery that it was more important for them to stay together despite their economic circumstances. For some reason, Renee couldn't get Jeffery to believe that money was not important.

Renee wondered how she would be able to make the $1,000 mortgage payment with only one income. She thought about several of Jeffery's friends who also worked at the plant. Some of them reacted just like Jeffery did, but others were trying to go on with the rest of their lives. Renee pondered about why men react differently than women to their economic circumstance. She imagined what life would be like if the plant had remained open. She smiled for a moment and considered her response when asked what was the reason for the divorce. She would say, "The plant closing and relocating to Mexico." Renee wondered if this was the real reason and asked, "Jeffery, why is it that men have such big egos? I didn't marry GM or the Fortune 500; I married you. Won't you please come home?"

♥♥♥♥

Darryl was sitting at the bar working on his sixth drink drowning himself in his misery. Earlier that evening, he came home and found a note on the kitchen table from his wife, Kathy, who had decided that she needed to find herself. It also said that she was bored and wanted to do more with her life than simply work from 9 to 5, and clean up after him from 5 to 10. Kathy's note went on to say that things were not the same anymore between them and that Darryl no longer made her happy.

As Darryl sipped on his rum and Coke, blasting in the background was *Midnight Train to Georgia.* Darryl wondered if Kathy was on the train with someone else. Was that the reason why she was unhappy? Deep down inside Darryl knew that was not the real reason.

The bartender asked him earlier that evening why was he feeling so low, and Darryl replied that his wife had just left him. The bartender asked if there were any indications that this would happen, and Darryl answered no. But then, Darryl began to replay the events of their four-year marriage in his mind. There were times when Kathy wanted him to help out around the house, do the dishes or, every once in a while, prepare dinner.

Darryl couldn't believe that a marriage could dissolve over who did the dishes and who cleaned the toilet. Kathy was always a complex person. She had the ability to be a lawyer, but had been working as a legal secretary. She had often said she wanted to go back to school to complete her undergraduate studies and pursue a law degree. She knew it would be hard work, going to school and taking care of the major domestic responsibilities. Darryl thought, "I guess that was supposed to be my clue - that she did not have to work and that I would help out around the house." But he didn't offer to do those things, and he didn't know why. Maybe he didn't

11

think they would have enough money without Kathy's salary. Or maybe he was afraid that she would become smarter and find someone else who also had a law degree. Darryl liked things just the way they were. He liked coming home and relaxing until dinner was served.

Darryl wished that Kathy would come back, but he wasn't quite sure that he could make her happy. He didn't know if anyone could make another person happy. Darryl knew that he was OK with the relationship, but maybe that was because he was able to do what he wanted. He did know that he would rather be at home with Kathy right now than in this bar by himself. He wondered where Kathy was right now.

❤❤❤❤

David was having a very difficult time becoming sexually aroused with Donna, his wife of fifteen years. It just wasn't the same. Sex had become a ritual every Tuesday night at 10:30; the variety just wasn't there. Seventeen years ago, when they were dating, Donna was the finest sister you could imagine. David used to call her "double take" because every time she walked by a brother he would have to turn around and do a double take. They still called her "double" because she was now twice as big as she was seventeen years ago. Donna swore that you couldn't have three babies and stay the same size, but David knew better. He had seen several women have children, and return to their natural size. It had nothing to do with the children; it had to do with all of those cakes and cookies she'd begun to eat, and not using all the exercise machines she'd bought over the past ten years.

It was easier for David to have sex with Donna only if the lights were turned off and he did not have to look at her, but he could still feel the flab. David will never forget once Donna told him "you're not the same brother you were seventeen years ago either, you've got a little pot belly and some handle-bars on the side." That was true, he was 164 lbs when they got married and he's around 194 lbs now. But it was different, David just couldn't get as aroused as he used to. He didn't have any problems with getting a little excited looking at some magazines or an x-rated video; hey, whatever it takes to get it up.

What really got David about Donna was when he told her that they needed to try some new positions; seventeen years of him on top needed to be changed. Donna went along for a little while and they altered positions but one night when David asked Donna to engage in oral sex with him, she flat out refused. She wanted to get into a discussion about how did he even know about oral sex. David played it off and said he had seen it on a video, he didn't know if she knew he was lying, but David really knew because he had learned first hand from Deborah, with whom he was having an affair.

Deep in his heart, David didn't really want to be with Deborah, he wanted to be with Donna, the one he had known seventeen years ago. Donna had no intention of performing oral sex, she wanted to continue the discussion and swore that David knew how it felt because he had experienced it with someone else. Here he was trying to get some sexual satisfaction and now they had to have this discussion, which of course developed into an argument.

So David being the man that he was, simply walked out, went over to Deborah's house and got what he wanted. All Donna had to do was get with the program, and they would not have any problems. David doesn't understand why the marriage had to break up simply because he wanted Donna to lose a few pounds, get rid of her sexual inhibitions, and deviate from the Tuesday-at-10:30 routine.

♥♥♥♥

"Lamont, you ain't nothing but a self-centered, low-life dog. I wish you would pack your bags and leave. You ain't nothing and your mama ain't nothing 'cause she spoiled you rotten. I don't want our sons to be anything like you!"

Denise had a lot of time to think about everything she had told Lamont after he left. She didn't know why she had said things that she really didn't mean. Denise didn't want Lamont to go. The words just came out.

Denise had read all the books that said to never indict a person, but do express dissatisfaction with his/her behavior. But Lamont had made her so angry! Once he had Denise and the kids waiting (with bags of groceries) for over an hour, and all Lamont had to say for himself was, "I got tied up." Tied up my foot, Denise thought. When Lamont did arrive, he tried to explain why he was late, but Denise didn't even remember what he said. All she knew was that she and the kids had been waiting for him outside of the grocery store for over an hour.

Lamont probably wanted to leave in the first place and was looking for an excuse, and Denise gave it to him by telling him he could leave. She wished he would come back because Denise had a few more things she'd like to tell him. It's hard talking about somebody when he/she is not there; it's like trying to argue with yourself.

14

Sometimes he just made her so doggone mad! When he did come home Denise would tell him she was sorry, give him a little lovin' and try to make up. Lamont needed to understand that if he was going to be late, he needed to call her in advance. All Denise wanted Lamont to do was communicate with her and let her know what was going on. Lamont always said that she talked too much. Denise wanted to talk about the problem before it started, while it was going on and after the problem was gone. Lamont said all women did was talk, talk, talk, talk, talk. Denise believed all men did was walk, walk, walk, walk, walk.

Denise didn't know why she told him he could leave! That was stupid; she knew she would have difficulty living without Lamont. She couldn't pay the bills without him, or raise their three boys by herself. Denise would bet that Lamont was having the time of his life. But she was going to get on his case when he came in here. Leaving her like this, ain't that something! Most of the time when she told him to do something, he didn't do it; then she told him to leave, and he was out the door.

They did not have a communication problem. Lamont did what he wanted, exactly when he wanted. If it was about him doing everything that Denise said, they wouldn't have this problem. Denise told him to pick her up at 5:00, and he didn't do that. She told him to leave, and he did.

They had a selective problem; Lamont selected what he wanted to hear and what he didn't want to hear. Maybe Denise should just keep her mouth shut when she's around Lamont, let him do all the talking. And if he had nothing to say, then they simply would not talk. When Lamont came home

Denise was going to try and be quiet and see if that would keep them together.

♥♥♥♥

Sandra and Robert have been married for the past seven years. They met in graduate school where Robert was working on his MBA, and Sandra was finishing law school. They discussed the possibility of starting their own consulting firm down the road, but first they both just wanted to get experience, pay some bills and make a lot of money working in corporate America.

Robert worked for a Fortune 500 firm and knew he had the potential to become a Vice President, maybe even the next CEO if he played his cards right over the next twenty years. Sandra worked for a big eight law firm.

Both Robert and Sandra were one of the few African Americans in their departments. Often their White colleagues would tell them that they were different. Robert and Sandra both knew that was racism coming out. It wasn't so much that they were different as much as this was a White stereotype. In order for Whites in the office to maintain their level of racism, they had to make Robert and Sandra honorary White citizens.

Corporate America began to put a strain on Robert and Sandra. They both worked long hours and had to deal with the pressure of evening dinners, cocktails and golf outings with their White co-workers. There was also frustration over salary differences. Robert knew that he was not making as much money as some Whites with similar educational backgrounds. Sandra found out that there were people who were not even attorneys making more money than she was.

16

Robert and Sandra both left their home early in the morning and returned late in the evening. Sometimes Sandra left at 5:30 a.m. and didn't return until 9:30 or 10:00 at night. When she did get home, she read legal briefs and prepared herself for the next day. Often Robert would complain that he didn't have a wife, but he wasn't much better because he worked almost as long as Sandra and sometimes had to travel two to three days a week.

Sandra's mother once asked her if she was married to Robert or her job. Sandra didn't respond because she felt she was married to both. One day Sandra counted how many hours she spent with Robert and compared them to the hours she spent at work, and the totals weren't even close. The job won easily.

One particular evening, Robert was in the study reviewing an acquisition proposal and Sandra was in the living room on the sofa reading a legal brief. It was 10:30 p.m. and, ironically, they were both thinking the same thing: "Do I want to be married or be the CEO?" They also wondered if it was possible for an African American (particularly a female) to become a major officer in corporate America. What price would she have to pay in order to find out? They both decided independently that after eight years of elementary school, four years of high school, four years of college and three years of graduate school and the possibility of making a million dollars a year plus stock options, they were going to find out.

♥♥♥♥

Patrice had tried to ignore the sad fact that Michael, her husband of fifteen years, was addicted to cocaine. It's understandable why Patrice would do that; they had three wonderful children, a beautiful home and everyone thought they had it all together. Michael was a good husband, an excellent provider and he loved spending time with his children.

Over the years, however, Patrice began to notice that Michael's alcohol consumption was increasing. She never imagined that Michael's intoxication was also a result of cocaine usage. When they first got together, Michael would drink a beer every once in a while and hold a drink throughout the evening in social settings. Sometimes if Michael was feeling good he would even have more than one, but it seemed liked everyone drank socially. There just didn't seem to be any reason for concern.

Michael had always said there would never be anything that could control him because he had too much discipline. He thought he was strong enough to monitor when and how much he drank. Michael underestimated the power of cocaine. Cocaine is not like alcohol, it takes all as prisoners.

It was difficult for Patrice to find out just how extensive the problem was because Michael made so much money that she didn't really miss $250 here or there, especially since Michael frequently worked overtime. But Patrice did notice that Michael began asking her for money in the grocery store when he had always been the one to pay the bill.

For over two years, Patrice chose to ignore the fact that her husband had become seriously addicted to cocaine. She looked around her church and community and realized how hard it was for couples to stay together. She and Michael were compatible, in love and still good lovers.Everything was right in the marriage, except his cocaine usage.

Patrice began to tell her girlfriends that she

could compete against another woman, but she knew she could not compete against his career, another man or cocaine. Patrice wondered how the children would react if she left. She asked Michael on several occasions to seek counseling, but Michael believed he could control cocaine like he had controlled his social drinking for the past twenty years.

♥♥♥♥

Kofi and Imani have been married for the past three years. Theirs was one of those ready-made, blended family arrangements, and Kofi and Imani were determined to make it work.

When Kofi met Imani, she had two children: a thirteen year-old son named Kevin and an eight year-old daughter named Cherise. Kofi used to marvel at the fact that Imani had told Kevin several years ago that he was the man of the house. Kofi used to debate with Imani on whether it was biologically possible for an eight year-old boy to be the man of the house. Imani always responded by saying that before Kofi, Kevin was the man of the house because she wanted to make him feel important. He was Mama's little man.

Mr. Johnson, Kevin and Cherise's father, visited once a month and dropped off whatever "guilt money" he could between jobs because he did not pay child support.

Kofi and Imani had an excellent three years together. They were best friends, worked together and were both unselfish lovers. The greatest challenge to their marriage was the rearing of the children. Kofi said he never would forgive Imani for telling him, "You don't love him like I do," after he chastised Kevin. Kofi didn't know which was worse,

Imani's statement or the children who frequently reminded him that he was not their Daddy. Kofi shrugged off the children's statements because he understood that children will say anything to get their way, even turn two biological parents against each other. Surely, they would try to play off the emotions of a biological parent and a stepparent.

Kofi never liked the term "step" because he always felt that parenting was more sociological (especially for fathers) than biological. He wondered how it was possible to earn the distinction of father purely by procreation. Why was the man who paid the bills and put food on the table called "step" and someone who visited once a month and dropped off a little money called father? He also wondered why every Black woman he had dated who had children became so defensive about them, especially their sons.

Tonight Kofi stormed out of the house because he felt that it was three against one. Kofi knew what he was getting into when he chose to marry Imani. He knew that children who have been with one parent for a long period of time form bonds that are unbreakable and sometimes unhealthy.

Imani always said that she was working on trying to share the discipline and parenting, but it was difficult sharing that responsibility after having been alone with Kevin and Cherise for so long.

Kofi wondered if they were going to be able to stay together. He regretted that even with all they had going for them they were in an unbearable situation. He did not want to live in a house that was divided.

♥♥♥♥

Linda and James had only been married for six months, and the relationship was already strained.

Linda recently told her girlfriend, "I wish we had lived together before we got married because then I would have realized that as much as I love James, we just don't have similar life-styles. Even though both of us like bowling, tennis, movies, travel and we are compatible in bed, we are just too different." Who would have thought of considering divorce over toothpaste?

People laugh when they mention things like toothpaste, but it's difficult being married to some-one when the life-styles are incompatible. Linda thought the toothpaste should be used and put away, while James thought it should be kept out because it was used so frequently. Linda was a day person while James was a night person. James was a vegetarian while Linda had no problems consum-ing a plate of chitterlings. Linda enjoyed quiet evenings at home reading a book, and James enjoyed playing his stereo for the neighborhood to hear. Linda felt it was easier to clean up after yourself while James felt shoes, socks and pants could be left anywhere and picked up at the end of the week since the house was going to be swept, dusted and mopped anyway.

Who would have ever thought that a marriage would be affected by such little things? But as Linda herself said frequently during their brief marriage, it was the little things that people had to deal with day by day.

Linda still felt she made the right decision by keeping her morals and not living with James before they were married. But she wondered how she could have found out any other way that you could love someone and not be able to live with them. Going out to concerts and to dinner did not give you an opportunity to discover everything.

21

Linda laughed to herself and remembered that whenever she visited James at his apartment, it was always neat. "I guess I always came over after he had cleaned," Linda said. She wondered what she would tell the judge: "I love him but I don't like him," or "I can't live with him because I think shoes and toothpaste should be put away, and there is a time for solitude, and there's a time for volume."

♥♥♥♥

In the next chapter we are going to analyze the issues reflected in these eight scenarios: economics, self-esteem, sexual relations, communication, racism and sexism, drug abuse, blended families and incompatibility as well as in-laws. These issues will be analyzed from a macro perspective.

We seem to have it so "together" in public, but behind closed doors, some of the statements and behaviors that are displayed defy all forms of logic.

♥ CHAPTER III

RELATIONSHIP ISSUES

The divorce rate is 50 percent among Whites in the United States, and 66 percent among African Americans.[1] Some people would even estimate it to be as high as 80 percent. The additional 30 percent is comprised of those couples who are separated and are no longer living together but legally never got the divorce. These figures do not include the marriages that remain intact statistically and legally, while emotionally, they have not been "together" for years.

In Africa and in more traditional settings, the divorce rate is between five and ten percent.[2] It is becoming harder and harder for Americans (particularly African Americans) to stay together. When divorce figures reach this magnitude, the problem may not lie solely with the individual couple, but it may be that culture and society make staying together very difficult.

In the previous chapter, we observed individual couples and some of the experiences they encountered. To impress upon you the magnitude of this problem, let me ask you to pause right now and name five happily married couples (other than your parents) who have been married for at least five years and are under forty-five years of age. For many people this assignment is very difficult to complete.

The leading factors that seem to cause the greatest havoc in male/female relationships or marriages include: economics, lack of self-esteem, lack of spirituality, sexual compatibility, lack of communication, the issue of power, various forms of racism, classism or sexism, drug abuse, stepparenting and in-laws.

Please note that in this chapter the quality of a relationship cannot be discussed if the numbers are not present (i.e., the male shortage). This issue is so very significant that the next chapter will look exclusively at the male shortage and its impact on male/female relationships.

As a writer, it has been frustrating for me to observe how we seem to have it all together in public, but behind closed doors some of the statements and behaviors that we express defy all forms of logic. We know theoretically how we should relate to one another, but oftentimes, we seem unable to do so. There have been things that I have done or said behind closed doors that are so reprehensible, no one could ever imagine that Dr. Kunjufu would have conducted himself in such a manner. That's why I mean it very sincerely when I say I'm not writing this book for you; I'm writing it for me. All of us (if we are honest) must admit that some of the things we have said and done are not commensurate with our age, maturity or educational background. It has been said that no one can get on our nerves like the person to whom we are married. It has also been said that we relax around loved ones, and that may explain why we sometimes treat strangers better than we treat our mates. In new relationships, we are trying to make an impression. That is no longer a necessity in an existing relationship. If we do treat strangers better than our mates, that is unfortunate because our mates deserve better.

All of the issues that we are going to discuss could lend themselves to individual books in their own right. The first issue is the economic pressure on relationships. In the previous chapter, we saw that Renee and Jeffery had been happily married for many years. Unfortunately, the impact of Jeffery's plant closing and the relationship between self-esteem, manhood and economic self-sufficiency was enough to transform Jeffery into a different man from the one Renee had known and loved.

This first section on marital issues will look at the impact of finance. Not only will we discuss the adequacy of our economic resources, but we will also discuss the values that are used to disburse these resources and who controls them. Economic pressure in relationships is by no means a new concept. In 1920, 90 percent of African American children lived with their fathers. In 1960, about 80 percent of African American children lived at home with their fathers. In the 1990's, the number of African American children living with their fathers has dropped to a low 38 percent.[3] We would be naive if we thought the problem in male/female relationships was purely based on personality conflicts. This tremendous decline in family stability directly parallels the changes in the economy from agriculture to manufacturing to high technology.

We saw in the second chapter how difficult it was to stay together when economic resources become scarce. Many couples are unable to marry because they believe marriage requires some initial income just to propose. Fifty-five percent of all African American males whose annual salary is less than

26

$5,000 feel unqualified for marriage.

I often tell couples that planning the wedding ceremony will test their compatibility because they will have to express their respective values in terms of the economic resources they each want to be allocated for the event.

What does a couple do when one spouse wants to spend $300-$1000 on a small wedding ceremony, while the other spouse wants to spend $3,000-$5,000 on a larger ceremony? There is a legitimate argument that since the wedding is only going to take place for one day, the money should be saved and used as a downpayment on a house, car, furniture or some other long-term investment. The counter argument is that a wedding is the event of a lifetime, the one and only time the individuals plan to get married, and there is no need to be frugal.

In his book, *Black Masculinity*, Robert Staples points out that if a man chooses not to marry, he could literally spend $70,000 dating.[4] This could explain why more and more brothers expect sisters to take *them* out, or at least share the expenses. Many brothers simply elect to just stay in for the evening watching videos together.

In a capitalistic society where money is a means of exchange as well as an expression of power and self-esteem, money becomes the vehicle through which many of our values are expressed. Money also becomes a means of control. One of the major issues in male/female relationships is money; not only how and why it is spent, but who controls it.

A great deal can be determined about the compatibility of a couple based upon their spending patterns. Do they have a joint checking account? Are there any hidden savings accounts? Do they put their money into the pot together? Are statements made such as, "This is my money, and I'll do what I want to with it?" Even when there are separate accounts, does a third account exist only for the good of the household?

Historically, since men have been the major breadwinners, they oftentimes feel that they should be able to control all of the movements, life-style and expenditures of their spouses. As more and more women begin to move into the work place earning as much if not more money than their husbands, this equality creates greater tension between men and women -- if these couples allow themselves to be defined by their income.

Later in this chapter we will look at the impact of power, racism and oppression on relationships. We will also analyze in further detail the impact of institutional racism on African Americans of the lower median income as compared to their White American counterparts. Probably the areas where trust in relationships is scrutinized the most are finances and infidelity.The ability of couples to trust each other on financial management issues is significant. Consider that one-third of the African American community makes less than $5,000, or is unemployed. These conditions are hindrances to our finances and our relationships. On the other hand, we do have 25 percent of the African American community earning over $40,000 annually.[5] Some of these African Americans have become economically self-sufficient, and are able to work at home. In addition, there are now 750,000 Americans of all races who are involved in commuter marriages.[6] This jet life-style has some African Americans living in separate cities and flying to be with each other on weekends.

Another major factor affecting male/female relations is self-esteem. Many times in relationships one party will say, "He/she did not make me happy." The assumption here is that their happiness is predicated on the behavior of their spouse. Many people sincerely believe that if they change partners they can enhance their self-esteem. I take the fundamental position that no one can make you happy; that is always your responsibility. You should consider yourself fortunate if, within a seven day week, your mate can give you a reasonable amount of joy for one or two days. Many single people believe that their unhappiness is due to the absence of a mate; therefore, securing one will provide a remedy to all of their problems. In contrast, many married people believe if they were by themselves, they too would be able to regain that initial bliss.

Maulana Karenga, in the book *The African American Holiday of Kwanzaa*, points out that there are seven levels of unity which include self, family, neighborhood, community, nation, race and world. Many of us have attempted to move to the second level of unity (family) without mastering the first level (self).[7]

In our concluding chapter on solutions, we will offer Frances Welsing's theory 28/30/2/4 which speaks directly to the relationship between self-esteem and spouse-esteem.

Many of us have an unrealistic view of marriage. Several articles indicate that our expectations of marriage are twelve times higher than they were in previous generations.[8]

> It [marriage] was not originally created as an institution designed to provide personal happiness.Until the twentieth century the family was an economic unit in which the arm of production was lodged. Along with

group production of goods and services came the reproduction of children, sexual access, and socialization. Love and happiness were afterthoughts which came to full expression in the twentieth century. Those qualities have to be sought and worked out by a conscious and joint effort. The imperfections of most humans will forever make their achievement a challenging task.[9]

This trend originated in a narcissistic society where ego (edging God out) has become supreme. There are benefits and disadvantages to this elevated state of expectations. It is true that many marriages in the past were maintained for less than ideal reasons; many couples stayed together solely for the children or because they did not have the economic options to leave. We need not be naive and assume that just because a couple has been married for twenty to fifty years also means that they are happy. At the same time, we need not take the position that momentary unfulfillment justifies leaving our mate in search of greener pastures. There is a need to draw upon the rich tradition of our past and seek a higher level of commitment in our relationships. At the same time, we do need to demand more of our spouses than simply fifty years, regardless of quality.

Many people believe that one of the best ways to maintain their relationship or marriage is to give up their individuality and immerse themselves into the life-styles of their mates. It is a sad tragedy when someone who liked to sew, read or play a musical instrument, or engage in any other hobby or activity forgoes these interests so they can do whatever their mates desire. We must always remember: we came into the world single, and on the day of judgment, our lives are reviewed singularly, and that is the way we will leave.

Kahlil Gibran, in a beautiful poem on relationships, describes the need for spaces between each other.

Then Almitra spoke again and said, and what of marriage, master. And he answered saying: You were born together, and together you shall be forever more. You shall be together when the white wings of death scatter your days. Ay, you shall be together even in the silent memory of God. But let there be spaces in your togetherness, and let the winds of the heavens dance between you. Love one another, but make not a bond of love: let it rather be a moving sea between the shores of your souls. Fill each other's cup but drink not from one cup. Give one another of your bread but eat not from the same loaf. Sing and dance together and be joyous, but let each one of you be alone, even as the strings of a lute are alone though they quiver with the same music. Give your hearts, but not into each other's keeping. For only the hand of life can contain your hearts. And stand together yet not too near together: for the pillars of the temple stand apart, and the oak tree and the cypress grow not in each other's shadow.[10]

Over time, people who lose their individuality also lose a large part of themselves. It is very difficult to feel good about your mate when you're unactualized and unempowered.

I have noticed in my own marriage that when my wife Rita has had an enjoyable conversation with a friend or a relative or has experienced an enjoyable program or activity, she is a much better wife to me, and I'm sure she would agree that I'm a much better husband under similar circumstances. If for none other than selfish reasons, it behooves all mates to encourage their spouses to fulfill and pursue their own interests. The better they feel about themselves, the more they contribute to and enhance the relationship.

One of the anecdotes in the first chapter described an individual solemnly stating the need to find himself/herself. Many of us have created the illusion that we have needs that must be fulfilled in order for us to be happy. Research indicates that five of the most frequently mentioned needs that males share in a relationship are the desire for sexual fulfillment, recreational companionship, physical attractiveness, domestic support and admiration. Women expressed that their five greatest needs are affection, conversation, honesty and openness, financial support and family commitment.[11] Pause for a moment, and ask yourself what are the five greatest needs that you desire in a relationship. If you are in a relationship, ask yourself if these needs are being met. One of the things that cannot be emphasized enough is that your needs do not have to be the responsibility of your mate.

Another marital issue that deserves a great deal of discussion is the issue of sexual compatibility. It has been said that marital financial management and sexual relations reflect the quality and value of the relationship. If a couple is open, honest, giving, unselfish and communicative with each other, this will be reflected in how they relate in bed. If there is a degree of selfishness in the relationship, this can also be exposed in the bedroom.

Many men often say that they want their women to look the same; but for many women this becomes very difficult. Many men married their wives when they were 21-25 years old, weighed 110 pounds and were 36-22-36. Ten to twenty years later, and after having three children, many women are not able to maintain their former weight and dimensions. Many men use this change in appearance as rationale for going outside the relationship, even

32

with their own sagging bellies and handlebars.

Another issue surrounding sexual compatibility is the frequency. Seldom will you find two people with the exact same desire. Interestingly enough, most people enter marriage thinking they will be sexually active three, five or seven days a week; numerous studies point out that the average couple has intercourse between one and three times a week. Often the frequency is based on or affected by job schedules, energy levels and the sharing of domestic responsibilities.

Many women feel it is difficult to be sexually aroused with someone who expects them to work, make dinner, wash the dishes, take care of the children and clean the house. And after all of this, their husbands want to make love. Often women have expressed resentment at being placed under this type of regiment and said if the responsibilities had been shared, not only would it have given them a greater appreciation for their mate, but reserved some sexual energy. Many married couples have resorted to the "Tuesday-at-10:30 syndrome" because the spontaneity is no longer there. By the time domestic responsibilities and children have been addressed, it is now 10:30 and time for the weekly ritual. According to Dr. Dan Kiley, when it comes to withholding sex, most women have a rationale that is impeccable:

> One woman said, "If he forgets to call me when he is going to be fifteen minutes late for dinner, I am just not in the mood for lovemaking. Maybe if I am not in the mood enough times, then he will get the point and start being more thoughtful."[12]

Dr. Dan Kiley continues by explaining the use of sex as a manipulation device.

33

> The woman's hollow view of herself as a sexual creature is confirmed; her ability to enjoy sex is decreased; her restlessness and longing are increased, as is her anger, and her bitterness toward life is focused on her man, locking her in a pessimistic view of love.[13]

In the last chapter we will read what the Lord has to say about sex being used to negotiate and manipulate.

The other area of sexual compatibility is the quality of the interaction. Historically, women have faked orgasm not only because they wanted to stroke the male ego, but also because of their own low self-esteem in not expecting or demanding equal fulfillment from their partner. The popular phrase in female circles is, "When he's through, we're through."

Again, one of the best ways to determine the quality of the relationship is if both partners are committed to trying to fulfill the other partner. Men need to know if their women have been sexually fulfilled, and women need to try to satisfy their men as much as possible. One of the more recent phenomena between men and women is the use of different techniques and positions during intercourse. Many men and women express the desire for oral sex, which can sometimes create tension in relationships. Often women will want to know why men want this, and they begin to question the trust in the relationship. They wonder if he experienced it outside of their marriage. A recent study by Battelle and Wayatt indicated that 93 percent of White women and 55 percent of Black women say they have experienced cunnilingus. Ninety-three percent of White women and 65 percent of Black women said they had engaged in fellatio. The fig-

34

ures for men are just as revealing. Seventy-nine percent of White men reported performing oral sex while 81 percent reported receiving it. For Black men, 43 percent said they had performed oral sex while 62 percent reported receiving it.[14]

Many couples have now become so concerned about technique, position and oral sex that they have missed what my father referred to as the third stage of sex. According to my father, phase one is foreplay, phase two is the actual act and phase three is a spiritual union. This is in strong contrast to putting a bag over a sister's face or performing phase two completely in the dark; they have no emotional or spiritual attachment to the person that they just entered. My father taught me a long time ago that as good as phase two is, it means nothing if you cannot advance to phase three, where you can look in each other's eyes with love, admiration and feel the presence of the spirit.

Beyond the issues of frequency, technique and compatibility the other major factor is infidelity or the inability to trust your mate in the relationship. Studies indicate that 75 percent of all men have at one time or another been involved in an affair while women are at the 50 percent level and rising.[15] With the imbalance between males and females, many social scientists and lay people are wondering if it is man's nature to be involved in more than one relationship or are the present-day societal standards responsible for this phenomenal increase in infidelity.

The next marital issue is communication. Many marital counselors indicate that the lack of quality communication is the primary reason for divorce. In the chapter on solutions, a great deal of attention will be focused on improving communication between partners. Often when we think of communication, we only think of the outgoing message. Many times communication problems are not the result of a lack of shared information, but the result of a lack of listening between the partners.

Is there a relationship between death rates and marriage? According to a recent study conducted by Princeton University, unmarried men have significantly higher death rates than married men. The average death rate for unmarried women was one and a half times that of married women. One explanation for this is that people with partners cope better with today's stresses because they have someone with whom to share their lives. Often single people complain about being alone, saying how empty their lives are and that no one really listens.[16]

James Walker, in his book *Husbands Who Won't Lead and Wives Who Won't Follow*, indicates that women are more supportive in conversation:

> When listening to a conversation between spouses, several startling differences appear. A woman gives both verbal and non-verbal support as the man talks about himself. The husband appears to listen less attentively and seldom asks his wife to discuss experiences. A man will often interrupt a conversation that involves women. In a group of men or women the conversation is matched and well paced and interruptions are kept to a minimum. But a mixed group is frequently interrupted by a man. Women often open the conversation with the leading question as many have mastered the use of queries to draw that out of people. Questioning is a distinctive ingredient of female speech. Women also hear emotionally; men tend to hear only the facts. Because the aspect of relationships is often an afterthought to men, they have difficulty mixing facts with feelings or seeing the emotional consequences of what they do.[17]

In Denise and Lamont's case from the previous chapter, Denise, like so many of us, said things she did not mean. Denise really did not want Lamont to leave, but in a moment of anger that is exactly what she communicated. It becomes imperative that partners only say what they mean; this takes a great deal of maturity. The acid test of whether you really meant something is if you can repeat that same statement twenty-four hours later. Many of us would love to be able to retrieve some of the statements that we have made to our mates. In male/female relationships, no one knows our weaknesses, frailties and insecurities any better than our mate because of the intimacy of the relationship. Unfortunately, in anger many people make harsh statements that can rupture the relationship indefinitely.

The first place a communication breakdown shows itself is in the bedroom. Things left unspoken by a wife will be in her thoughts during sex, and the husband may not understand the icy distance. In the chapter on solutions we will not only talk about the skills of listening and other techniques to improve communication, but we will also highlight the importance of indicting the *behavior*, not the *person*. Just as in our workshops on discipline between parent/child or teacher/student, it is very important that the person making the criticism attach the criticism to the behavior and not to the person. Often in parent/child or male/female relationships we make our indictment of the person, which makes the recipient defensive, rather than making the observation that the action was wrong but the individual is not a bad person. Key words to avoid are <u>always</u> and <u>never</u>.

Many women feel the major problem in communication is that African American men simply do

37

not tell the truth. Claudette Sims, in the book *Don't Weep for Me*, makes the following observations about some men and their habitual nature to lie:

I'm not married. Although you see the imprint of a wedding band and guilt is dripping off his brow into his courvosier.

When asked how did you get lipstick on your collar he replies I don't remember my secretary must have slipped and I caught her. There are eight sets of lips on his shirt apparently the tramp needs brain surgery or a good chiropractor.

You know I love you baby. This may or may not be true depending upon the time, the place and how hard he is. Have you noticed these six words are more frequently used while he's screwing you or after he's screwed up.

I don't know who she is. After he and some lady had danced the last nine dances and you've gotten wallpaper sores from standing in a corner fighting off creeps at a party you didn't want to go to in the first place. He may not have known who she was when she came in, but you can bet that he'll know her name, number and favorite position before she leaves.

This has never happened to me before baby. After that unfortunate attempt to get it up. This has never happened to you before when, yesterday, last week, since the sixth grade, what are you the incredible hulk? Give me a break we're both adults. You have a problem let's talk about it. It's not the end of the world unless you think with your penis and not your brain.

I'll call you tonight or tomorrow take your pick. This is a classic one, sound familiar? These lines are usually spoken in passion or minutes after you've made out. More often than not in your home in your bed. Men rarely say it when you leave them alone in their bed the morning after. Something about being in their own domain that makes them feel they don't have to make any promises to anyone.

I stopped by a friend's house right after work and he didn't have a phone. After getting off work at five o'clock and getting home at two a.m. you have a friend that doesn't have a phone. What is he a neanderthal man? Everybody with lips has a phone.

I'll be back in a few minutes, I'm going to get a pack of cigarettes. Four hours later he strolls in empty handed smelling like a distillery and wonders why you're pissed.

I'll do it in a minute. After you ask him to take out the garbage, pick up his stinky socks, hang up his shirt, take his plate off the table or wipe the toilet seat.

She doesn't mean a damn thing to me. You're overreacting after you caught him having a drink in a bar with a half-naked girl thirty miles from home at four o'clock in the afternoon. Or God forbid in your bed with a fully naked girl when you decided to go home for lunch unexpectedly at noon.[18]

While a major issue in communication is male honesty, many African American men respond that when they are honest African American women are unprepared to handle it. For example, many men point out that after the second date with a woman she will ask if he is seeing someone else. Before he can even answer, she also says that she has decided to date him exclusively as a result of two dates. Now she is expecting a similar response. I don't think the problem here is lack of communication; I think it is an unrealistic expectation and the desire to be exclusive has been made prematurely. Many brothers have indicated that if they answer the question honestly, she is unprepared for his answer. Many brothers say that if a question is going to be asked, people should be prepared for all options. You wonder if this is merely a question or an ultimatum and the development of a contract.

Some brothers who desire to refute the notion that Black men do not tell the truth have chosen to answer the question forthrightly by saying that they enjoyed her company, but are seeing several other women because they do not want an exclusive relationship. Often the response is disappointment, rage, tears, a slap in the face and walking out. Please appreciate that I am not endorsing lying, but I think it is unfortunate that exclusivity is introduced prematurely and that men feel they might lose the lady by telling the truth. Consequently, some men begin the pattern of lying. I'm encouraging women to question how early they want to initiate an exclusive relationship and be prepared for either response without incriminating the relationship.

The problems of communication are manifested in numerous ways. Primarily when individuals make polemic statements about the other gender. I had major problems with Shahrazad Ali's very controversial book *The Blackman's Guide to Understanding the Blackwoman,* but I believe that in every situation there is something to be learned. I thought Ali made some excellent points about the statements that some women are making about some men. (Note that I used the word some which Sister Ali did not use; authors need to avoid generalizations.) These are a few of them, and I would like for brothers to indicate how many they have heard from women:

- Shut up, you don't know what you're talking about.

- Why don't you mind your own business?

- You're such a mama's boy.

- You ain't nothin', and you ain't never gonna be nothin'.

- You don't tell me what to do.

- You do what you wanna do, and I'll do what I wanna do.

- Get it yourself.

- You think you're right all of the time.

- I get tired of you trying to tell me what to do.

- Why don't you act like a man?

- You're full of s_ _ _!

- That doesn't make any sense.

- Don't give it, unless you can take it.

- You didn't have nothing when I met you.

- Your family ain't s_ _ _, and you ain't either.

- Men are dogs.

- I do what I want to do.

- I might, and I might not.

- Why don't you hush?

- Be quiet!

- Shut up!

- You so stupid.

- You can't do that.

- Leave me the f_ _ _ alone!

- You mess up every time.

- I go where I want to go.

- It's my money, and I'll spend it anyway I like.

- You get on my nerves.

- It ain't your baby anyway.

- I told you so.

- My mother said you wasn't no good; I should have listened to her.

- You'll know payback when you see it.

- If you don't somebody else will.

- You can't do nothin'.

- Stop.

- Get out of my face.

- I don't want to hear that.

- Get out!

- I don't care what you do.

- I am tired of you.[19]

As much as we talk about communication problems which include lack of listening and honesty, these comments show total disrespect for each other. I also would like women to ask themselves if they have made any of these statements to men.

I think that the previous statements are important for women to review. I would be remiss and sexist if I did not ask men to ask themselves if they have ever made any of these statements:

- I'm the man of this house.

- Where's my dinner?

- Can't you keep a clean house?

- Nobody wants to be with you.

- You don't look as good as you used to.

- Why are you so fat?

- Fix yourself up, you look like a tramp.

- You think you're fine with your high yella a _ _ .

- You must be horny.

- A real woman knows how to make love to me.

- A real woman knows where to kiss me.

- You know you can't live without "this."

- I'm the best thing that ever happened to you.

- Take your kids with you.

- Look b_ _ _ _, come here, or I'll slap the hell out of you.

- You wanna be the man of the house 'cause you ain't never had a daddy.

- All you women are just alike, you just want the money.

- So you think because you make more money that I can't pay the bills?

- You think you're smarter than me because you got a degree from the White man's school.

- You need to quit staying at the church all day taking care of the pastor and come home and take care of your family.

- You need to quit talking to your mama all the time.

- You need to quit talking to your girlfriends all the time.

- B_ _ _ _, I'll kill you.

- Don't play with me.

It is amazing the things that we say behind closed doors. People with degrees, church folks, people committed to the liberation struggle and people who appear to have it all together, myself included, would be greatly embarrassed if the world got a chance to see a video tape or hear an audio tape of some of the things we say behind closed doors. All of us need to review this list and honestly ask ourselves if we have made any of these statements. This is just the tip of the iceberg.

Shahrazad Ali goes on to point out that women are taught to say these things by their mothers. Listed below are some of the statements mothers teach their daughters as they prepare them for male/female relationships:

- I don't care what your father said, I said . . .

- I've got to cook and clean up this house before your father gets home 'cause I don't wanna hear his mouth.

- Your father don't run this house, I do.

- He don't know what he's talking about.

- He don't know that I know.
- He don't know what he's doing.

Later on as girls become teenagers, they may experience the following situations:

- A warning from the mother about not telling the father how much an item of clothing really costs.

- Not letting the father know that the mother had an accident or forgot to pay an important bill.

- Not letting the father know the daughter is dating prematurely or came home late from a date.

- Not letting the father know the daughter is on birth control.

- Keeping quiet about the daughter failing a test to prevent her from being punished or grounded.

Later on, the daughters will get their last set of instructions which may include the following:

- Get a good education so you can get a good job and take care of yourself so you won't have to count on no man.

- Make your own money so you can be your own boss.

- You know you can't trust him so be careful.

- All men want is to get in your pants.

- Play the field for a while, find out what you want.

- Don't believe just what he tells you, check him out.

- Don't let him get you pregnant.

- You can't tell a man all your business.

- Don't spend your own money, make him pay for it.

- Make him do something for you, don't spend all your time with him for nothing.

- Get with the one who's got the most money.[20]

It should be obvious that we are going to have problems in male/female relationships if daughters are receiving a diet of these statements regularly from their mothers. Mothers need to review this list and ask themselves if they are guilty of using any of these statements. If so, this needs to be corrected.

In the spirit of fairness, we should also provide a list of some of the statements fathers and mothers have given their sons in preparation for male/female relationships:

- Boys will be boys.
- Sow your oats while you can.
- All women want is your money.
- Don't ever show your true emotions to a woman.
- Don't marry her just because she got pregnant.

- Be careful, she don't have a daddy at home.

- Women respect you more when you cheat on them and slap them around.

- That's my boy, he didn't mean to get you pregnant.

- That's my boy, he didn't mean to steal from your store.

- That's my boy, he didn't mean to kill anybody.

Before leaving the area of communication, let's deal with some classic statements we share with each other that are so ludicrous and tragic they become humorous:

- A married man will often ask a woman, "Honey, you married?"

- A man who is tired of dealing with his own children will ask a woman, "How many kids you got?"

- A man will fool around with another woman, get caught and ask his wife, "Baby, what *we* gonna do now?"

- Women in the same circumstances will say, "He caught me at a bad time. I was vulnerable."

- When a woman has been shacking with a man for six years and when she finally mentions marriage he says, "We don't want to rush into anything."

- You know things are dangerous when one

47

person says, "Honey, we need to talk."

- When it is time to break up, the classic statements are, "We'll always be friends. It's not that I don't love you, I just need time to think and I have to find myself." [21]

When I was sharing the rough draft of this book with a friend, she mentioned that we have to find a way to reach our youth on male/female relationship issues. That is why I am requesting that you pass this book on to a young person. Studies indicate they become sexually active between 11 and 14, but parents do not begin discussing sex education with them until they are 16. As a result the rappers, videos and x-rated movies are communicating to our youth on this and other vital subjects. Listed below are some of the statements that have caused African American females to lead the world in teen pregnancy.

- If you really love me then show me.

- You act like a baby.

- If you really are a man/woman then make me feel like a woman/man.

- I promise we won't go all the way, unless you want to.

- I'll stop whenever you say.

- I want to marry you someday, but we should find out if we are sexually compatible.

- Everybody is doing it but us.

- Don't worry, you can't get pregnant for the first six months; God gives a grace period.[22]

Between the ages of 11 and 14 when some of these teenagers' parents are not discussing sex with them, many teenagers are making their own discoveries through their peers and the media. Other major issues affecting male/female relationships are the areas of oppression, sometimes referred to as racism (overt and institutional, i.e., white supremacy), sexism or classism. All of these terms involve the same basic issue of power and control.

Racism plays a major role in our perceptions of each other in male/female relationships. Many of us still possess a Eurocentric definition of beauty. I often ask brothers what criteria they use to determine if a sister is fine. During many of my workshops I often raise the question, What is the definition of good hair or pretty eyes? Many of us talk Black but have a Eurocentric definition of beauty. If beauty is defined as long hair, blue eyes and light skin, then racism has once again affected our definition of beauty. A regular dose of Hollywood movies has taught us that White females are very submissive, passive and supportive of their men. As a result, many African American males expect African American females to act like White women. Not to be outdone, many African American women want their men to act like White men - to buy them a house in the suburbs, two cars and vacation in Orlando once a year.

Neely Fuller writes that "until you understand white supremacy, then everything else will confuse you."[23] Many of us underestimate the impact that racism has had not only on our individual pursuits, but on the stability of our relationships as well. Racism shows its ugly head in every aspect of our lives, whether it be in employment, promotions, income, housing patterns, standard of beauty or the expectations that we have for each other. As mentioned earlier, it is very difficult to feel good about your mate when you do not feel good about yourself. Racism saps self-esteem.

In my book, *Black Economics*, I indicated that the median income for African Americans is 61 percent of the median White income. The African American family could benefit from a 39 percent increase in income. If African Americans earned the same amount as the median White family, the Black community would receive an additional $127 billion. Each billion dollars generates 30,000 jobs, which translates into four million additional jobs in our neighborhood.[24] This provides greater stability and allows more men to consider marriage.

Do you know what it's like to have greater qualifications than your co-workers but have to train someone less qualified to be your supervisor? What must it feel like to leave work and return home every evening to face your spouse after this scenario?

Beyond the impact that racism has on relationships, sexism is equally severe. One of every two husbands physically abuses his wife. There are 800,000 incidents of rape reported nationwide among all races each year, and only one in ten rapes is reported. In actuality, the total number of rapes each year is estimated to be approximately eight million. The issue of date and marital rape is seldom discussed primarily due to male privilege. Marriage and the church may be the only two bastions where Black men wield power. Many Black women have been told by their husbands either at knife or gun point, "I will kill you before I let you leave." My pastor, Jeremiah Wright, postulates that the same married pastors who deny women the opportunity to preach are the biggest whore mongers in the church. Sexism expresses itself in numerous ways, from some rappers who cannot produce a complete song without calling Black women b_ _ _ _, to the words that many brothers use to describe their sexual exploits, which include: ram, screw, jam, pop, knock, ride and bang. Numerous articles have been written by African American women describing their disdain at walking down the street or through the park because of the distasteful comments they receive from brothers. Many sisters under these circumstances have studied their options. They can ignore the brothers and be considered stuck-up, or respond in a negative way and be called a b_ _ _ _. Many have decided its best to smile, ignore the comments, and just walk away.

Sexism is an illusion that insecure men use to rationalize to themselves that their differences make them better. As a result, in male/female relationships, if a female has a college degree she has a 10 percent greater chance of divorce. If she had one year of graduate school, the chances of divorce go up to 15 percent. If she has two years of graduate school or pursues a Ph.D., the rate increases to 19 percent. The following chapter on the shortage of Black men discusses how many females anguish over the possibility that if they go back to school or secure a promotion, they are reducing or eliminating their chances of securing a mate. In contrast, when African American males increase their educational status or secure a promotion, they become more marketable, another illustration of sexism.

Professor John Kinney of Virginia Union points out that in an African value system $1+1=1$, but in a European value system $1+0=1$. This anecdote was shared early in the book, and it encompasses the issue of empowerment. The 1 symbolizes the individual in the relationship who has the most power, and the 0 represents the person with no power. When people who are secure with themselves are comfortable marrying people equally as secure, then $1+1=1$. People who are insecure are not comfortable marrying people who are empowered. They look for people who are insecure and unempowered because they are comfortable with $1+0=1$.

However, these representations of relationship power may not always remain stagnant. Throughout the course of marriage, individuals grow and develop. This causes tension in some relationships because a marriage based on $1+0=1$ runs the risk that at some point the 0 may begin to stand up for him/herself, which will result in tension. The good news is that 0's don't always remain 0's, and the other person is forced to make an adjustment. A female friend commented that she had once been a 0 and her husband loved it, but once she became self-actualized, educated, employed, had her own money and car and demanded that her husband participate in child rearing and domestic responsibilities, he could not handle it and they sought a divorce. When he kept insisting that she return to her former wonderful self, she responded very candidly, "That b_ _ _ _ is dead."

Most of the favorite phrases in my marriage come from my wife, whose very presence demands respect. Her favorite cliche' is, "This is Rita." When she says this, the meaning is clearly understood. It means, "I can think and speak for myself, and I do not need you to do any of that for me." If someone asks me if they can meet the two of us for dinner on a particular day, I could not speak for both of us because *I am not Rita*. It means that in any situation she has 50 percent of the marital vote and 100 percent as it relates to her participation.

Many Black men, including myself, are "recovering sexists." I live in a world based on male privilege, and I am often reminded of that. I appreciate this opportunity because it is not my desire to take advantage of anyone else. Being married to Rita allows me to grow even when I feel like resisting.

Bill Cosby masterfully illustrates the dynamics of power in a relationship:

> If any man truly believes that he is the boss of the house, then let him do this: pick up the phone, call a wallpaper store, order new wallpaper for one of the rooms in his house, and then put it on. He would have a longer life expectancy sprinkling arsenic on his eggs. Any husband who buys wallpaper, drapes, or even a prayer rug on his own is auditioning for the Bureau of Missing Persons.[25]

The next issue that we want to address is the impact that drugs have on our relationships. Unfortunately, cigarettes and alcohol are drugs that are sold and used in America so casually they have become national pastimes. Many people truly believe they can control their alcohol consumption.

In my book, *Hip-Hop vs. MAAT*, I indicated (to the surprise of many) that the leading drug killers are not heroin and cocaine, but alcohol and cigarettes. The comparison of these two types of drugs were not even close. Heroin and cocaine each kill less than 10,000 people. Alcohol kills 100,000 and cigarettes, 435,000.[26] Yet many people continue to look at alcohol and cigarettes as casual drugs that can be controlled and regulated. Many of us naively believe that we drink and smoke because we want to, and our habits have nothing to do with the influx of billboard advertisements and the large number of print ads in Black magazines.

In the previous chapter, we showed the impact that drugs had on Patrice and Michael's very stable marriage. Many brothers really believe that their drug problems can be controlled. Many sisters do not know what to do in this arrangement; therefore, they are unable to provide their husbands or sons with tough love. The illness not only affects the user, but all other family members as well. It becomes important that the drug users receive help, which can only be accomplished when they acknowledge that they have a problem. Initially, the spouse must help the user to admit that he/she has a problem and then direct the person to the proper sources to receive help. Unfortunately, there is a great deal of denial among both parties. The user, therefore, will not leave, and the remaining spouse does not provide tough love. I have seen families literally destroyed, not only because of the drug abuse (and the physical abuse that often accompanies it), but also because of the financial abuse that develops to maintain the addiction.

The next issue we will look at is the number one problem affecting second marriages, stepparenting or blended families. In many cases, adults who have come together for the second time are older, more mature and have realistic expectations of marriage. Unfortunately, because most did not do it God's way, they now have a ready-made family where children are already in existence. Blended families are unique because of the age of the children, gender and personalities and the involvement of the non-custodial parent. There are some blended families where this parent is not active, but in others this parent is active and may have a different child-rearing agenda than the stepparent. Some blended families only have children from one spouse, while in other blended families the children come from both spouses. Some children live in the home full-time while other children visit. There are even situations where children come from both spouses and they both stay in the blended family. The other parent may or may not be involved on both sides of the equation. The biological parent may tell the children that they do not have to listen to the blended parent and/or the non-custodial parent. This creates a triangle of confusion and places a tremendous strain on relationships. It is very important that, before adults agree to a blended family arrangement, the issues of child-rearing, discipline, money management, jealousy and egos be thoroughly explored.

Another major variable that affects blended families is the number of years that the children have been with their parent before the marriage. There is no question that it is easier to have a blended family if the child is younger and has had fewer years alone with their biological parent. Many adults also tell me that the opposite sex attraction is a variable to be considered. You might think that the new male in the family would have a greater chance of bonding with a male child as opposed to a female child, but sometimes that is not forthcoming. If a boy has been taught that he is the man of the house, there may be some degree of competitiveness for the attention of the mother. This could be a major problem if mothers have given their sons everything. Men often say to other men that mothers are very defensive about their sons.

Another major factor to be considered in blended families is the area of discipline. Many biological parents would prefer that the blended parent simply provide a nurturing environment and economic resources, but that discipline should be distributed by the biological parent. It is very difficult for an adult to be in a household where he/she does not have the right to discipline the children. As I mentioned earlier, I do not speak and write books just for my audience but for myself as well. Rita and I have experienced many challenges raising our children in our own blended family.

Often the child/biological parent bond is greater than that of the newly formed couple. Many children have seen potential and actual spouses come and go; some are even allowed to recommend or choose the spouse. The biological parent has always remained. It becomes imperative that adults commit themselves for the long haul and not allow children to create instability in the marriage.

The next issue we need to look at that affects relationships is incompatibility. In the previous chapter, we mentioned that Linda and James loved each other dearly and expected a successful marriage, only to find that marriage was more than dating and concerts, but a merging of life-styles. For many people this becomes difficult. Seldom do adults discuss their views on child-rearing, housekeeping, savings, furniture, sleeping patterns, etc. I have known couples who were on the verge of breaking up over snoring that had become unbearable for the other spouse.

The issue of cleanliness is a component of incompatibility. Obviously, the person who values cleanliness the most will have the greatest problem adjusting to someone with a lackadaisical attitude about housekeeping. Ninety-four percent of married women say they do more work around the home, and the men agree. Surprisingly, however, only 21 percent wish the men would do more around the house.[27] A major conflict women have as they expand their career pursuits is that they are not sure they want to give up the thing that has always given them self-esteem - the ability to take care of their home and family.

A successful marriage requires not only that you love and like each other, but that you are able to live with each other as well. I will never forget an older couple that had been dating for years. I wondered why they never married, and one of them told me that they had become too settled in their ways and it was better for them to enjoy each other's company by dating. When it was time to go home, each person went to his/her own individual house. Katherine Hepburn once said that men and women should just be neighbors and visit each other occasionally, as opposed to committing to a lifetime relationship.

The last issue which is still a major factor in relationships, but has been declining over the years is the impact of in-laws. Ironically, the greatest problems come more from the female side of the family than the male. Seldom will you find a father-in-law creating havoc in a relationship; it is usually the mother that we see portrayed as demanding on television. Many sons are still able to return home to their mothers, but if their fathers were there this would not occur as frequently. Many mothers remain the primary influence on their daughters.

Another issue with in-laws is the dynamic of grandparenting. Many times grandparents do not respect the rules of their children and allow the grandchildren to do whatever they want. Often in-laws still believe that their children should do what they say regardless of what their grown child wants them to do.

♥♥♥♥

All of the issues discussed in this chapter could have severely adverse affects in your male/female relationships. In order to begin lowering the alarmingly high divorce rates mentioned earlier, these issues should be among those that are discussed *prior* to the marriage ceremony.

*Is it possible for brothers to be faithful
with the present male shortage?*

CHAPTER IV

WHERE ARE THE BROTHERS?

* African American men feel the greatest challenge facing them is economics.

* African American women feel their greatest challenge is trying to survive without a husband and father for their children.

> Then the king of Egypt spoke to Shiphrah and Puah the two midwives who helped the Hebrew women. When you help the Hebrew women give birth he said to them kill the baby if it is a boy. But if it is a girl let it live.
> *Exodus 1:15-16*

> When Herod realized that the visitors from the East had tricked him he was furious. He gave orders to kill all the boys in Bethlehem and its neighborhood who were two years old and younger - this was done in accordance with what he had learned from the visitors about the time when the star had appeared.
> *Matthew 2:16*

Throughout history, there has always been a plan to kill male children. It has been said that one of the most effective ways to find out what God values is to monitor Satan. It is obvious that God values family. Satan is aware that one of the most effective ways to destroy the family is to kill the male. How can the family procreate and grow if there are no males? Satan comes in many forms whether it be the king of Egypt, Herod, White supremacy, the Fortune 500 or the Trilateral Commission. There has historically been a concerted effort to destroy the male child, especially the male child with the most color, i.e., the African male child.

Listed below are some tables describing the male shortage.

Sex Ratio of the Nonmarried Black Population 18 Years and Over: 1972, 1977, 1982, 1987

Sex Ratio for Total Population

	1972	1977	1982	1987
Male	2,490,000	3,221,000	4,144,000	4,645,000
Female	3,893,000	4,827,000	6,060,000	6,699,000
Sex Ratio	64	67	68	69

Sex Ratio by Age

Year	18-19	20-24	25-29	30-34	35-39	40-44	45-54	55-64	65+
1972	101	96	63	64	48	71	46	47	38
1977	93	90	79	59	44	54	64	55	43
1982	95	93	81	65	73	48	55	53	34
1987	93	93	86	78	63	65	47	60	35[1]

These tables are primarily provided for those who require quantitative empirical data, preferably from White sources. However, brothers and sisters in the "hood," without University degrees, can already articulate the gravity of the Black male shortage.

These figures, compiled from the US Statistical Abstract, have several inadequacies. First, they never include our entire population, specifically those who are homeless, unemployed, without a

YEAR AND SEX	Total all Years	Under 5 Years	5-9 Years	10-14 Years	15-19 Years	20-24 Years	25-29 Years	30-34 Years	35-39 Years	40-44 Years
Black										
1980	26,495	2,436	2,491	2,673	2,985	2,725	2,321	1,889	1,458	1,251
1990	29,986	2,786	2,671	2,602	2,658	2,579	2,708	2,682	2,337	1,876
Male	14,170	1,408	1,350	1,314	1,342	1,259	1,286	1,251	1,083	866
Female	15,816	1,377	1,321	1,287	1,316	1,320	1,422	1,431	1,254	1,010

YEAR AND SEX	45-49 Years	50-54 Years	55-59 Years	60-64 Years	65-74 Years	75 Years And Older	5-13 Years	14-17 Years	18-24 Years
Black									
1980	1,143	1,129	1,037	871	1,341	746	4,596	2,364	3,914
1990	1,406	1,179	1,033	962	1,503	1,005	4,784	2,014	3,712
Male	642	532	457	414	618	348	2,418	1,023	1,825
Female	763	647	576	547	886	657	2,367	991	1,887

African American Males over the age of 18 in 1991

Total 9.3 million

Single	3.7 million 40%	Married	4.3 million 47%
Widowed	0.3 million 4%	Divorced	0.9 million 9%

African American Females over the age of 18 in 1991

Total 11.4 million

Single	3.9 million 34%	Married	4.7 million 41%
Widowed	1.4 million 13%	Divorced	1.3 million 12%

Source: US Statistical Abstracts 1992 [2]

Social Security number and are not involved in any aspect of government. Secondly, these figures only require that the men be alive, regardless of their legal, employment, educational, health, geographical location, military status, sexual persuasion, interracial desires or sanity. Lastly, tables that attempt to measure the marital status in the African community will be inaccurate. I have mentioned previously that the divorce rate is 50 percent officially but swells to 80 percent unofficially because many African Americans separate but never officially divorce. We will not even speculate whether the US Statistical Abstract can measure the number of African Americans who are shacking, which I call playing or practicing marriage.

The University of Chicago estimates that by the year 2000, 70 percent of African American males will either be unemployed, in jail, on drugs or dead. The figure rises to 80 percent if we include African American males in interracial marriages, those who are mentally ill or homosexual, all of which makes males unavailable to women.[3]

What can our community do to prevent so many African American males from being lost to the above situations? The process of rites-of-passage from boyhood to manhood to husbandhood to fatherhood and elderhood is a process that many African American males never achieve. Listed below are some of the obstacles that I have outlined in my bestsellers *Countering the Conspiracy to Destroy Black Boys Volumes I-IV.*

- Infant mortality
- Failing kindergarten
- The fourth grade syndrome
- Disproportionate numbers placed in special education

- Mothers raising their daughters and loving their sons
- Disproportionate numbers suspended
- Overemphasis on athletics
- Teenage pregnancy
- Drug abuse
- The drop-out rate
- Disproportionate numbers in the military
- Double digit unemployment
- Homicide
- Suicide
- Homosexuality
- Interracial marriages
- Disproportionate numbers in prison
- The lowest life expectancy

Infant mortality in African American communities exceeds rates in many economically underdeveloped nations worldwide. For a myriad of reasons African American males die disproportionately to their female counterparts. In 1991, 20,000 males died at birth compared to 17,200 females.[4] The male shortage for many females began before they left the hospital.

Some of us might not have been aware that when teachers disproportionately fail more Black boys between kindergarten and third grade, there is a 70 percent chance they will not graduate from high school and a tremendous possibility that they will not matriculate through the rites-of-passage into husbandhood and fatherhood. Every African American female and concerned adult needs to be mindful that the five to six year old little boy who failed kindergarten was someone's future husband and father. This act at the tender age of five or six is robbing the African American family.

Who would imagine that the issue of African American male/female relationships could be affected by a school district that has low expectations for the African American male child and does not realize that children learn in different ways and mature at different levels? This same analysis applies to the decline in academic achievement scores for African American males after fourth grade and the disproportionate number of African American males placed in special education and suspended. Again we raise the question, who would imagine that issues such as the decline in academic achievement after fourth grade and the preponderance of female teachers to place African American male children in special education could affect African American male/female relationships?

Eighty-five percent of the African American children placed in special education are male.[5] This has implications for adult African American male/female relationships. Adults can save the next generation of male/female relationships by monitoring the academic achievement of African American males. If they do not matriculate through the system, there is little hope that they will become responsible, economically stable citizens.

In many large urban areas, the dropout rate for African American youth hovers near 50 percent, especially the African American male child. Alvin Toffler's *Third Wave* describes an economy in which the first wave was agriculture, the second wave was industrialism and the third wave was high technology and computers. It is very difficult for African American males to access this "third wave" if they do not have a high school diploma. A class of freshman students entering high school is fairly evenly divided between males and females, but at the high school graduation, the numbers are heavily skewed towards females. I have seen entering Freshman classes of 1,000 students, 500 of whom are male and 500 female. Four years later at the graduation ceremony, only 500 students graduated; 350-400 of them were female with the remaining 100-150 being males. What are the marital possibilities for the 350-400 African American males who did not graduate? Will they be able to provide the kind of nurturing, protection and economic support that their wives and children need?

Young people are living examples of the lack of association between their dreams and their reality. When I speak across the country to youth groups, I always ask the youth what they will be doing when they are 30 years of age. Over half the males answer that they are going pro in one of the major three sports, with the top choice being basketball. Presently, African Americans comprise 86 percent of the NBA starters. The sports industry is valued at over $90 million with only three percent being allocated to its players. The remaining 97 percent are white collar positions and those with careers that exceed the average player's five years.[6]

Whenever I am in small towns in the South (which is known for producing large numbers of athletes), I often try to determine the number of brothers who thought they were going pro, and what they are presently doing. Some of the stories I have heard are tragic. There are numerous African American males that are between the ages of 23 and 35 hanging on corners in towns I have visited. These brothers were one step away from a million dollar contract, and when they did not make it, they were not advised to take academics seriously. So they are now hanging on corners, washing dishes, waiting tables or performing other menial services for minimum wage. Now there is a tremendous disparity between their million dollar dream and their $4.35 reality.

We have to wonder what type of relationships these men provide to their women and children. We also have to raise the question, Would things be different if they had a teacher, parent or a coach who required academics before sports? Could things have been different if they had studied the same amount of time they played ball? Would things have been different if they had played a sport where the money was not as lucrative, i.e., swimming, wrestling or track?

The next area we need to discuss is, mothers who are raising their daughters and loving their sons and the impact this has on male responsibility, teenage pregnancy and male/female relationships. Some mothers will make their daughters come home early to study. They teach them domestic responsibility and take them to church, yet they do not require any of this from their sons. In the following chapter on how to select a mate we will look at the implications that childrearing has on male/female relationships. I do not believe that you can be an irresponsible man unless you were allowed to be an irresponsible boy.

This lack of accountability for males in childhood often carries over into adolescence and adulthood. Ninety percent of teenage pregnancy programs counsel the females, thereby absolving the male of any responsibility.[7] The classic statement that boys will be boys is only true if we let them.

There are several macro factors affecting relationships, including the deleterious effects on unemployment. Those males who are no longer looking or applying for positions do not even exist in the U.S. statistical report. Some figures estimate that 60 percent of African American teenagers are unemployed, and closer to 30 or 40 percent of African American men are unemployed. In a patriarchal, capitalistic society based on White male supremacy it is very difficult for a man to be a man without an adequate source of income.

Violence in the African American community has reached a critical stage. Homicide is the leading killer of African American males between the ages of 13 and 35. It is no accident that between the ages of 21 and 35, a period when males should be the most productive economically, African American males continue to be the least productive. In the African American community, if we can keep our males alive until the age of 35, there is a very good chance that they will become productive husbands, fathers and elders. However, African American males who desire to be more productive are denied the opportunity because our capitalistic society is based on White male supremacy. So, many African American males believe they only have six options: NBA, rap, drugs, crime, the military or McDonald's.

Morris F.X. Jeff calls the dynamic between the homicide rate and the unemployment rate for males between the ages of 18 and 35 *entropy*.

Entropy is a stage where a unit of the system, void of its essential maintenance resource, i.e., energy, is deprived of the capacity to carry out its subscribed function. At this juncture the unit begins to disintegrate randomly and ultimately dies. During this death process, the disintegrating unit causes havoc as it becomes the hostile force, arbitrarily, capriciously and spontaneously bombarding other units quite often causing damage and death to these units before ultimately succumbing itself.[8]

This clearly describes what is going on in the African American community. Many people feel there is a direct relationship between poverty and crime. If this is true, then African American women should be committing crimes more than anyone else because they are the least paid. The reality is that African American males want the same power that White males possess, especially during the time between the ages of 18 and 35. If unable to secure this power, entropy sets into the community.

The onslaught of guns and drugs in the African American community has major implications for adult male/female relationships. Studies report that 76 percent of all drug users are White, but 60 percent of all drug convictions are African Americans.[9] This is by design, it is not an accident. It is very consistent with the failure in kindergarten, the fourth grade syndrome, special education and suspension for African American boys. It reinforces White male supremacy.

African American males do not want to sell drugs. When given alternatives of selling Final Call newspapers, working at a plant, joining the military or having some other economic opportunity, they choose the latter options over the former. We need more African Americans to start businesses that will provide economic alternatives for our people other than selling drugs. We also need governmental policies that will stop the infiltration of drugs into this country, especially since

85 percent of all drugs come through South Florida, California and Texas. We need a government that will monitor banks that are laundering a $150 billion industry. We need a penal system that will realize that it is more effective to prosecute the drug user than the dealer. How can the latter sell if the former no longer exists? We need governmental policies that will allocate more money for treatment than for enforcement. Fifty-five percent of all users want treatment, but only 15 percent are able to receive it because 70 percent of the budget is allocated towards the penal system.[10] Maybe the government is not aware that going to jail does not curtail or eliminate a drug problem. We need more self-esteem development programs and a moral fabric in the country that will reduce the demand for drugs. There are countries where drugs are produced, but citizens do not use them. America does not have a drug problem. America has a moral, values and self-esteem problem. America suffers from material narcissism.

There are approximately 900,000 African American males in prison, and the number continues to rise. The United States of America sends more people to jail than any other country in the world. One out of every four African American males is currently involved in the penal system. The number of African American males in jail surpasses the population of some large cities. Can you imagine the impact that the 900,000 African American males in jail has on male/female relationships?

Many articles are now illustrating that African American females have chosen to become emotionally and intimately involved with inmates, many of whom have lifetime sentences. What is the alternative when 25 percent of our population is involved with the penal system?[11] The tragedy is that this can be prevented. Ninety-five percent of the males in jail cannot read beyond a sixth grade level. We could improve Black male/female relationships if we simply taught African American males how to read. Ninety-five percent of the African American males in jail do not possess a high school diploma nor did they ever receive one course in Black history or culture. Again, we could improve male/female relationships if we helped these men graduate from high school and taught them the truth about Columbus, Lincoln and Washington as well as Martin Luther King, Malcolm X, Marcus Garvey and Imhotep. Can you imagine improving the quality of Black male/female relationships simply by making school curriculums more Africentric?

Ninety-five percent of the boys in jail were on the corner between ten o'clock at night and three o'clock in the morning. Many African American males are at the wrong place at the wrong time when the police need someone to fit a crime description. Lastly, ninety-five percent of the boys in jail did not go to Sunday School, and did not confess that God was first in their lives.[12] If only mothers had made their sons go to church. If only pastors had a liberation theology and provided programs and activities for the youth and males of the church. If only churches had removed the image of Michelangelo's cousin representing Jesus in church, perhaps more African American males would have gone to church, and we would then be able to stabilize adult African American male/female relationships.

We also need to explore the fact that currently America has an 85 percent recidivism rate for penal

71

institutions.[13] There are other institutions, such as the Nation of Islam and progressive Christian churches, that have reduced the recidivism rate with inmates who join their ranks. Many states have dropped the word rehabilitation from jails and prisons because that is not part of the agenda. Many women have begun corresponding with inmates, who often respond with long, emotional letters, possibly because they have nothing else to do. I have heard sisters express greater satisfaction from these confined relationships than from brothers who are physically available. As African American women view some of the recent articles about becoming involved with inmates, they have to ask themselves if long-term commitment to inmates is a possibility for them.

The next obstacle for African American males is suicide. European males commit suicide more than anyone else, but African American males are a very close second and lead the nation in the critical age range of 18-35. It becomes very difficult to distinguish whether the cause of death was homicide, accidental or suicide. Many African American males in their prime have placed themselves in suicidal conditions. European women are third; African American women commit suicide less than anyone else. I wanted to investigate what makes African American women so strong, considering they are the least paid and often have children with no males present in the home. First, it was discovered that African American women cry releasing their negative energy at that moment, which avoids suicidal tendencies later. Secondly, African American women share their pain with friends, and finally, women give their pain to God. Many African American men do not cry, and they teach their sons not to cry. They are too macho to share their innermost secrets with another brother.

They feel it is a sign of weakness to confess God first in their lives.

I now want to tie this macho concept into the dynamic of homosexuality. It is not my desire to get into the moral ethics of, nor the genetic argument for, homosexuality. I still take the position that sin is sin and that Negro preachers who condemn homosexuality from the pulpit while trying to sleep with every woman in the church are being hypocritical. We should not be in the business of ranking sin. The only point I want to establish here is that homosexuality contributes to the male shortage for African American women. Unfortunately, many men who are open, honest and communicative are labeled sissies. Many men who want to pursue academics, music or the church are labeled less-than-masculine. This tension between mental and physical has made it very difficult for males of all races to find balance. I initially thought that African American women had a greater disdain for interracial marriages than homosexuality. African American women have shown me that when they lose a African American male to a White woman, they lose one; when they lose an African American man to another African American man they lose two. Often, these brothers are well groomed, well educated, like to cook, sew and clean. They are open, honest, tender and communicative, like to go to church and are good listeners, but unfortunately they prefer male companionship.

You might think that with a male shortage the greatest number of African Americans dating and marrying outside the race would be the group with the shortage, i.e., African American females. The reality is just the opposite. There is a 2:1 ratio of African American males to females who have married

73

outside of the race. There are 231,000 interracial marriages, with males consisting of 156,000 and females consisting of 75,000.[14] When I ask African American males why they chose to date or marry out of the race when they statistically have two to five women to choose from, I hear three popular responses: White women are more understanding, less demanding and are considered to meet the definition of beauty which includes a white or almost white complexion, long and straight hair and any color eyes but dark brown. I have attended college and professional athletic social gatherings where it appeared that the host had unloaded a bus of White females into the event. Many of these White females are aggressive and know exactly what to do to take the Black man from his African queen. At some of these functions, I found that several African American women were denied entrance, and others were disrespected by some of the brothers. A major economic drain to our community is the large numbers of athletes and entertainers who have married White.

The last factor creating the shortage of African American males is life expectancy. European women on the average live to age 77; Black women live to age 75; White men die at 71 years of age, and Black men die at 63.8 years of age. Studies show that African American men live longer when they are married, yet we see that there is almost a twelve-year disparity between Black men and Black women. Studies show that when men are not married they drink and smoke more, eat more fried foods, consume more beef and pork and have less tendency to secure regular medical checkups.[15] It is tragic to observe church populations and see large numbers of African American women 55 years of age and older who had successful marriages, but unfortunately are widows because their mates died prematurely.

The first part of this chapter has been an attempt to give a cursory overview of the plight of African American males. There are numerous books on the subject, including my own, that go into greater detail. I felt it was imperative in this book on male/female relationships that the quality of the relationship could not be discussed if the numbers were not present. If a basketball coach was attempting to fill a team and only five players tried out, the coach would have no other option than to start all five players. If an employer is looking to hire somone who can type 50 words per minute, has good communication skills and is a critical thinker, but only receives three applications with the best applicant typing only 28 words per minute with errors, having less than adequate communication and critical thinking skills, the employer would have to resort to hiring that person. The coach and the employer had to lower their expectations because of the shortage of qualified applicants. The players, the employees and some African American men have an over inflated image of themselves, which can prevent them from improving. The coach, the employer and some African American women subsequently place less pressure on them to improve.

I have heard stories that on college campuses, some African American males are literally interviewing sisters as if they really are the employer. The first question they ask is, What can you do for me? I mentioned earlier that every honest male in a sexist society must acknowledge that he has sexist tendencies and has to consciously try to overcome them. I am a recovering sexist, and just as a recovering alcoholic is only one drink away

75

from falling back into destructive behavior, I am one act away from sexist behavior. The same applies here, where African American males must do everything in their power not to exploit the circumstances that the imbalanced ratio provides. Many brothers tell me that it is not their desire to exploit this dynamic. They were dating exclusively or were faithful in their marriage and not looking for anyone but were propositioned. Many African American males know how to be the hunter, but have very little experience in being the hunted. Sisters, because of their tradition and upbringing, have been taught how to say no to advances. Many brothers are now going to have to learn this lesson as well. Some brothers have told me that even after refusing a proposition, the scorned women spread rumors they were gay.

Audrey Chapman, in her book titled *Mansharing*, raises the question, Is it possible for brothers to be faithful with the present male shortage? Monogamous women should monitor their men for the following behaviors:

1. He begins to go out more often by himself.
2. He calls less frequently.
3. After a whirlwind courtship, he cuts back on weekend commitments and opts instead for a night during the week.
4. He decides it would be better to meet at your place than his.
5. His night out with the boys stretches from late night to all night.
6. He fusses more with his physical appearance, maybe even changing his style of dress or brand of cologne.
7. He jumps when the telephone rings and rushes to answer it himself.

8. You noticed a marked increase in hang-up calls and wrong numbers.
9. His travel schedule inexplicably changes, and he is missing often from his work for long stretches of time.
10. Overtime at the office suddenly increases but when you call he's not there, or he claims he was somewhere doing research.
11. The frequency of sex diminishes, or he has a sudden interest in experimentation.
12. He starts coming home late and heads first to the bathroom to wash up instead of talking to you.
13. He moves further and further away from you in bed.
14. You notice more entertainment charges on credit cards, and he begins to have more trouble balancing the checkbook.[16]

The above situations are becoming more frequent in African American male/female relationships. There are brothers who realize they are the 30 percent that have survived the conspiracy and believe they are God's gift to women. There are women who, like the coach and the employer, decide to accept the slim pickings that are available. Just like the coaches and employers, there will now be competition among sisters for a piece of the diminishing pie. The arena of African American male/female relationships is greatly affected by the lack of unity that exists among sisters. The male shortage has created more backstabbing, disrespect and lack of unity among many sisters. I still naively take the position that real sisters respect the relationships of their fellow sisters. If a woman finds out that a brother is married or involved in a relationship, she should respect that relationship just as she would want another sister to respect her relationship with her partner. As a writer and a concerned member of the African American community, I have to raise the question, What are sisters to do in lieu of the male shortage? Do sisters in relationships have any responsibilities to their sisters without? In the following chapter on values, we will look at the issue of polygamy in which the African community recognized there was a male shortage and wanted to prevent the jealousy and backstabbing that could take place among women. They wanted every woman to have the opportunity to experience having a family and raising children and provided a mechanism for that to take place. What we now have to ask ourselves is, If women are not to share men with other sisters, what other options are available to them?

From reading numerous books and articles and conducting direct interviews with sisters, several options were noted:

- Date or marry other Africans who reside outside the United States.

- Relocate to areas of the United States where there are more African American men than women, primarily near military bases such as San Diego, CA, Norfolk, VA and Fort Bragg, NC. States with more African American or a close ratio are: Alaska, Hawaii, Montana, Wyoming, North and South Dakota, Colorado, Iowa, Vermont, Maine, New Hampshire, Arizona, New Mexico, Oregon and Washington.

- Expand the age range.

- Relax the income and educational criteria.

- Consider men from other races.
- Investigate serial monogamy.
- Explore lesbianism.
- Ponder polygamy.
- Utilize unofficial sharing.
- Contemplate political and rehabilitated prisoners.
- Remain single.

Each of these areas deserves a chapter, if not an entire book, in their own right. But the issue I want to highlight the most is being single.

As Claudette Sims reminds us:

> First and foremost let's get something straight right off the top, being single is not an illness or a disease. It is not contagious, or inflammatory. It is not a condition; it is a state, and the word single simply means not married. Being single means sometimes being alone, but being alone doesn't necessarily mean loneliness.[17]

The African writer Paul noted:

> Actually, I would prefer that all of you were as I am: [single]. But each one has a special gift from God. One person this gift, another one that gift. Now, to the unmarried and to the widowed I say that it would be better for you to continue to live alone as I do.
> *I Corinthians 7:7-8*

Single people have the opportunity to be unrestricted in developing their full potential and to become more involved in the liberation struggle. I see sisters who are married and unhappy, and I see others who are single and empowered. I also see sisters who are single and have returned to school, developed additional talents and have positive male and female relationships. They associate with men who are platonic, supportive and encouraging. I see these sisters involved in after school cultural awareness programs, rites-of-passage programs and other activities that make the African American community stronger. More will be said about this type of sister in the chapter on solutions. These sisters have chosen not to allow brothers to play games with them because of the male shortage.

In the next chapter we will look at the issue of polygamy from a values perspective. Another area mentioned was serial monogamy. While polygamy is illegal in America, unofficial sharing and serial monogamy are the order of the day. When juxtaposing one against the other, polygamy seems to be a better solution than unofficial sharing and serial monogamy. Within the context of a male shortage, this does not mean that sisters have not had the opportunity to be with, marry, and have children by a man. I stress that in a society with a male shortage, sisters will simply not have a man at the same time. Therefore, in the African American community, we have a situation where one brother over the course of thirty years has been married three times, spending five to ten years with each sister. Each sister has then had the opportunity to experience marriage and motherhood and now has a family with children, but no longer has a husband. What is the difference between serial monogamy, unofficial sharing and polygamy?

In America the first option, serial monogamy, is honest, legal, sinful, frequently used, beneficial for some males and provides instability to females and children. The second option, unofficial sharing, is dishonest, legal, sinful, frequently used, beneficial to some males and heartbreaking to most females. The third option, polygamy, is honest, illegal in America but legal in Africa, sinful to Christians but not to some religions, can be demanding and beneficial to most males and females, and provides family stability if there is cultural preparation and acceptance.

In this chapter, as we explore all of the ramifications of a male shortage and its impact on male/female relationships, we have to discuss not only the issue from a numerical standpoint, but qualitatively as well. There are many sisters who have taken the position that if they have a B.A., their man must also have a B.A.; if she makes $30,000, he has to make $30,000 or more also. Sisters traditionally and historically respond to the adaptive male. When females are younger and in elementary and high school, most respond to those males that have adapted to that environment. Those brothers that are athletes, well dressed, musically inclined, have a good rap, can fight and have the respect of their male peer group are the prize possessions for females of that age group. During this time those males that are considered nerds because they are successful academically, but are not respected by their peer group, are not the prizes for females.

Nathan and Julia Hare give the following insight:

Despite all the contemporary talk to the contrary women as a group appear in large part still to be guided by the longing for security and male protection. They are characteristically drawn to a man's social potency (his social position, wealth, prestige, power, intelligence) not merely his personal and physical charms. Paunchy old men with riches, power, and fame can emerge as wildly coveted sex objects while dashing male paramours without visible employment

81

or at least a convincing desire for same will ceremoniously be pitched out into the street despite the Black male shortage. The feminine attraction to the "adaptive male" complicates an already difficult situation. There are differences in what constitutes an adaptive male at different stages of a Black woman's life. Early in puberty, within the adolescent subculture of the ghetto, she encounters the most adaptive male in the form of the jive cat, walking tall looking mean talking clean "superfly character type." He knows he can dance and romance young women with enough rapping and cultivated pimpish mannerisms and maneuvers.

As a young or maturing woman seeking the mode of satisfactory love life with Superfly still dancing in the street hanging out in bleak pool rooms or iced away in prison, the young Black woman growing older tends to turn her attention to the once inept Booker T. Shy and withdrawn in adolescence, Booker T. had been inclined to spend inordinate amounts of time in the library or even the church house or other pastimes remote from the arena of adolescence courtship. But now Booker T. has become Mr. Booker T. Esquire unlike the undisciplined Superfly he now has a good, steady job. For all practical purposes, he may still be a square, but he suddenly seems sweet enough just talking like a banker and wearing a coat and tie and starch white shirt on a regular basis in broad daylight. Thus, many women may be impelled to live out their lives in an undying struggle to negotiate the duality of desiring Superfly and Booker T. both.

Meanwhile, the Booker T.'s of the world for their part, may remain perennially embittered by early female rejection. Seeking to save their injured adolescent ego, they may wrap themselves as adult men in a frenzied endeavor to make up for lost sexual time, coldly exploiting the middle class Black male shortage and their own new found appeal to the female multitudes now jilted by Superfly but liberated enough to pursue the adult world's most adaptive males. The Booker T.'s thus join the Superflys and even more daily varieties of males which the Superflys mimic.[18]

Valerie Shaw, in her book titled *Himpressions*, provides a brief description of the Booker T's and Superfly's who sometimes go by different names, such as the Benz-o-drivin' lady killer whose black book looks like the Manhattan yellow pages. Second is the professional man whose every sentence starts with I. Third is the career criminal or chronically unemployed. Fourth is the long-suffering, tormented alcoholic or drug addict. Fifth is the pathetic puppy whose luck just will not change. Sixth is the neat to the bone eternal bachelor, and seventh is the married to mama man or his cousin, the "my kids-can-do-nothing-wrong" parent.[19]

Now that we have a better understanding of the male shortage and its quantitative impact on Black male/female relationships, let's move into the next chapter on selecting a mate within that context.

The more selective you are in looking for a mate, the more time, energy, resources and skills you can bring into the courting stage.

CHAPTER V

SELECTING A MATE

I believe there is a science to selecting a mate. Unfortunately, most Americans spend more time choosing their cars, clothes, houses, colleges and majors than they do selecting a mate. The first part of the science is understanding the term "courting." Another aspect is looking for the evidence. Ask yourselves how long you were involved with your mate before you decided to marry him/her. How long were you involved with a person before you decided on an exclusive dating relationship? Is it possible that several weeks could provide enough evidence to decide on an exclusive relationship or marriage? There is the other extreme where people shack for years and never make the final decision to marry. There are relationships where many men have told the sisters, "I want to marry you," and after several years they still have not consecrated their vows. By and large most Americans, specifically African Americans, do not spend enough time in the court-ing process in order to secure the proper amount of evidence to make a lifetime decision. (I too had problems in that area.)

In *An Africentric Guide to Spiritual Union*, Ra Un Nefer Amen points out that Africans were very concerned about the selection process and realized that a decision of this magnitude could not be made solely by young adults. The community, specifically parents and elders, should be involved in the selection process. Ra Amen states:

> Due to the clear understanding that the internal commotion caused by the alterations and intraabdominal pressure that can make one hurt so bad to see one's loved one again does not translate into the ability to judge character - a skill needed to select a lifetime companion - the adults took this role upon themselves. After all, intrinsic to the definition of being young is the fact that one has not lived long enough to accumulate the information, maturity and experience necessary for such a task because the main support of the household will fall upon the male during the child bearing portion of the family's experience. This becomes the first and most important issue to be examined. Because of this, the first official step towards getting married is initiated by the young man who sends his friend with some money - a token of his earning ability to ask for the daughter's hand. His not going himself is an example of one of the many protocols created in African culture to establish and maintain respect, hence order in the society. A boy must defer, through socially prescribed protocols, to an older man's greater experience, maturity, and knowledge. How else can he be receptive to the guidance he surely needs for his development? If the daughter is interested then the father meets with members of his family, and the community looks into the boy's background as well as that of his family. Is he industrious? Did he pass his rites of passage; is he a hot head or is he amenable to counsel and discussion? Is there insanity or bad blood in the family tree? If they are satisfied then the young man's father is contacted and his family initiates a similar inquiry into the girl and her family.[1]

Most African Americans would consider these procedures extreme and far-fetched because we are too independent, mature and individualistic to allow anyone to be involved in the decision–making process of choosing a mate. Remember in America the divorce rate is officially 50 percent and hovers near 80 percent unofficially. It is obvious that there is room for improvement. We need to draw upon our African tradition to ameliorate the problem.

I know personally that I could have avoided divorce had my parents or a group of elders advised me. This explains why Frances Welsing recommends that we not even consider marriage until we are 28 years of age or until we have developed a strong level of self-esteem. There is a relationship between age, maturity and wisdom, and it may not be possible for a 16, 19 or 23 year old to make a decision with lifetime implications.

The need for other people to be involved in the selection process, for more time to be allocated to making the decision, or to spend the kind of time, energy and effort we spend in reviewing cars, clothes and houses as mates reinforces the fact that life has changed drastically over the past decade. Life was very simple for our parents and grandparents; they either bought a Ford or a Chevy, and ice cream came in only chocolate, vanilla and strawberry. Life is much more complex now, with 755 types of cars to choose from and ice cream is now available in over 33 different flavors. The same concept applies to individuals. If we ask our parents and grandparents how they met their spouses, they will probably respond in one of three ways: They lived in the same neighborhood, went to the same school or worked at the same location. Values were similar enough in that era to keep them together. Now individuals can live on the same block, attend the same school or work for the same company, but have a myriad of values and experiences within a similar age group. Some people will be Christians, Muslims, Jehovah's Witnesses, Buddhists, believers in Amen Ra, atheists or agnostics. Some people grew up in the South while others were raised in the North. Some will be committed to the race while others will be obsessed with BMWs, Mercedes and Louis Vittons. Some will love children, and others will not want to bring a child into the world. (I am glad their parents did not have similar views.)

Unfortunately, we now live in a world where people can be similarly classified by age, gender and race, but because of the myriad of values we now possess we can no longer rely on the criteria our grandparents used of school, residency and employment. Unfortunately, many of us are now using classified ads, dating or matching services. Magazines now have as their major editorial focus the matching of singles. This situation is particularly evident in large cities, such as New York. For example, a young man or woman lives in New York City along with 16 million other residents. He or she lives in an apartment complex with eight other units. Of the remaining seven, three are occupied by individuals outside of the race, two are of the same gender and the last two are unfortunately not appealing. The male or female uses public transportation to get to work each morning. Unfortunately, in large urban areas, people rarely talk to each other on public transportation, much less make eye contact. Therefore, despite the hundreds of people he or she could encounter on the bus or train, they probably will not meet anyone. He or she works in an office setting with sixteen other people; eight of whom are outside of their race; of the eight remaining co-workers, only four are of the opposite gender. He or she is interested in one of the four who consequently happens to be involved with someone else, so nothing happens. He or she then takes the bus or train home, and the same set of circumstances that were evident in the morning are reenacted in the evening. After arriving home, he or she reads the paper, watches the news, takes the dog for a walk, talks to a friend on the phone and takes a bath. This cycle happens throughout the week. On Saturday, they do their laundry, walk the dog, watch an afternoon movie and prepare to go to a party that night. The atmosphere at the party resembles a meat market and nothing results from this outing. Sunday morning he or she goes to church, but they are not members of any organization. After church they talk to a few people in the reception hall, but they really do not find anyone at church. As a result, they have gone through an entire week in New York City without finding a mate. For this reason classified ads, directories, magazines and matching services have now become big business in both the Black and White communities.

In researching and writing this book, I have been in touch with numerous agencies and editors for classified services. I interviewed them to try to ascertain their effectiveness. The overall result is that these methods have the possibility of being successful. If you find one person out of a hundred through these methods then it was worthwhile, especially if this person turns out to be the one you marry. Statistically, it has been ineffective for several reasons. Some respondents are married, vindictive and have hidden agendas not based on the principles of MAAT or Nguzo Saba. They play games and create grief in pursuing individuals through classified ads.

> The biggest pretenders are the pseudo-singles, that is, married men. By the estimates of black women, as many as 75 percent of the men found in certain gathering places are married. As a 38-year-old female researcher informed us, "When you go to some of these places and see all these men, you have to wonder why there are so many lonely black women. After asking around, you find most of them are married. There aren't many opportunities for single blacks to congregate in the same setting. A lot of married men are out looking for companionship, thus creating problems for single women." [2]

Another major response concerning classified ads is that many request that a photo be submitted with the response. When individuals do not send the photos and meet the other person based solely on the correspondence, they realize the "chemistry" is not there.

This issue of chemistry is paramount to the issue of selecting a mate. Unfortunately, one of the major reasons why many of us would not adhere to the advice of elders, parents and community leaders regarding the selection of our mates is the fact that the individuals making the selection do not have the same chemical formula that we have and desire in a mate. Another disappointing fact about this phenomenon of chemistry is that it is significantly affected by external factors. While many people say they revere and value friendship and intelligence, at the gut level, the most significant issue present when choosing a mate is physical attraction, which constitutes the bulk of this term "chemistry." Physical attraction has numerous implications. We live in a world with a Eurocentric value system that is influenced by the external. Therefore, we will encompass a European definition of beauty. Many terms that are often used in the African American community such as "good hair" and "pretty eyes" along with the value placed on light skin have had deleterious effects on African American male/female relationships. Robert Staples writes:

> Given that many Black men prefer their women light or White, the supply of such women is limited for a number of reasons. What, then, do Black males consider in their search for a desirable mate? A couple of surveys inform us on the question. When the Roper Organization asked Black and White men what qualities are most admired in a woman, the Black males ranked sex appeal fourth - White males rated it sixth. When Jet Magazine surveyed Black males in Chicago on the ten things they notice about women, they listed in this order: 1) face 2) legs 3) bust 4) eyes-hair 5) personality 6) dress and intelligence 7) smile 8) buttocks 9) walk 10) hands-feet-voice conversation-sincerity. More ironic is the fact that some of the desirable physical traits become liabilities over time. Big legs, for instance, often reflect a retention of fluid that can later cause kidney problems. People with white or fair skin may show signs of aging prematurely. Women with large breasts may find them sagging as they grow older. A woman's comeliness has its drawback for both men and women. The major problem encountered by men is that it has a ephemeral quality. The most attractive woman on a dinner date may not look as stunning the next morning sans her cosmetic accouterments. As men remain with an attractive woman over a period of time, her physical looks become routinized and subordinate to other qualities they rank as less important in their initial encounter. Beauty is also closely linked to a youthful appearance. If other qualities such as intelligence, emotional support, and sensitivity are absent or weak, the male who

is confronted with a beautiful but aging wife may feel betrayed and disillusioned in many ways and even disgusted with her reliance on charms which have faded with the passing of years. Still having found a "fox," they must cope with one of the most commonly heard complaints about pretty women: their narcissism. The eminent psychologist Karl Jung once remarked: "To me a particularly beautiful woman is a source of terror. As a rule a beautiful woman is a terrible disappointment. Beautiful bodies and beautiful personalities rarely go together." It is commonly known that men have a higher threshold of tolerance with pretty women. Hence, such women can, and do, demand all the market will bear: expensive gifts, deference, a delay of sex, etc., all things the less attractive woman can only dream about. Small wonder, then, that people with the same degree of attractiveness are more likely to stay together because the person simply feels more secure and comfortable with a mate of equal attractiveness.[3]

The issue of physical beauty is reflected in the attitudes of our youth. I enjoy speaking to young people; I remember once in Houston, Texas a brother raised his hand and said, "Jawanza, are you saying I need to marry some ugly sister?" I am not saying that, but I am saying that in a value system based on external factors, we belittle internal factors such as personality, communication, sincerity and friendship. The popular phrase, "ain't nothin' going on, we just friends," means just that. The reality is we would have much more stable relationships had we indeed married our friends. Parents and elders do not have our chemistry requirements, and that is why classified ads are not effective. They cannot quantitatively determine a person's chemistry. In the Western world, this can only be achieved based on the physical presence, which is based on a European standard of beauty.

Because we are all influenced by the physical presence we need to ask ourselves just how effective is a pretty face, a nice set of legs and a good shape in keeping a relationship together. When we look at the chapter on solutions, you will not find a pretty face, shapely legs and a slim figure as the ingredients necessary to reduce the divorce rate from 50 to 5 percent.

Unfortunately, in the Western value system, not only is friendship belittled, but the word "nice" is misunderstood. The word nice is derived from the Latin word *nescius* meaning ignorant: not knowing. The dictionary defines nice as pleasant, satisfactory, agreeable and delightful. The Thesaurus equates nice with agreeable, amicable, congenial and friendly. The word nice presents quite a dilemma for most brothers and sisters. Every normal brother or sister says that he or she is looking for a nice person, yet when they find a person matching this description he/she is treated like an unwelcomed guest. If the person develops feelings for you, you might not want to lose them, but at the same time you wonder why are they hanging around. Another problem with nice people is that it is tempting to do unto them as you have been done unto. If you have been jerked around by some heel, sometimes you just have to give someone else the boot. A nice person tells you that he or she is willing to wait forever for you to return his or her affections. You want to scream because that is exactly how long it will take. Men and women and the nice guys themselves all agree on one thing: nice people get no respect. Nice today means a brother or sister is gullible, stupid and conspicuously accessible. No wonder they finish last. Be honest. Where do nice people fit in with you?[4]

93

Often we camouflage our potential lovers by referring to them as friends. Many people feel that members of the opposite sex cannot be friends. I believe it is possible if the individuals resolve the sexual question with a formal discussion. Until the issue is discussed, the possibility of physical intimacy always exists. Secondly, if your opposite sex friend is really a companion, you should be able to share your joy and pain about your lover with this person. If not, quit fooling yourself and your lover.

Often we tell our friends that we cannot find a good brother or sister. We tell our friends what we look for in a mate but that is not what we choose. Many times the mates that we choose are based on our desire to be needed. We are trying to fill a void that was missing in our mother/child, or father/child relationships. Sometimes a financially secure person will marry a person who is in an impoverished condition. Later on the financially secure person will complain that the spouse did not bring any finances to the relationship. You will also find assured and confident people who will marry someone who is insecure and lacking in self-esteem. People will marry or date someone because of his or her rap or how they seduced them. In actuality, some of these same traits that were initially attractive may cause problems in the future. Being attracted to someone who is insecure, impoverished, a seducer, witty, strong-willed and defiant may be attractive initially, but may become a problem later on.

When I ask men what they are looking for in a mate, many tell me they want a woman who is independent and financially secure but someone who is sensitive to their needs. When I ask women the same question, they often respond that they want a man who is aggressive in his career but domestically compassionate. Many men do not see the contradiction in stating they want a virgin with experience. The complexity and contradictions in these requests are further indications of how severe the problems are in male/female relationships. Many popular radio stations across the country attempt to provide a dating service by asking the listening audience what they would like in a mate. Some of the more popular choices are: good looks, intelligence, a good sense of humor and the ability to have a good time. I want you to pause for a moment and ask yourself if you have any of those traits. If you do, all of you are eligible to win a mate on this radio station.

I felt this area needed an entire chapter because I believe that the more selective you are in looking for a mate the more time, energy, resources and skills you can bring into the courting stage. As Minister Farrakhan says, let the brother or sister make his or her case to convince me that it is worth giving my entire life to them. I do not believe that opposites attract, I believe that at the gut level like attracts like. I am willing to acknowledge that with any given couple, one person may be more extroverted than the other. One person may like the outdoors while the other may like the indoors; one person may like jazz and the other gospel; one person may like to read and the other may like television; one person may like to eat frequently while the other may watch his diet. I continue to believe that at the gut level, like attracts like concerning those values that represent the core of our being. These values are our relationship with the Lord, our commitment to the race, our commitment to our family and our values about money.

I believe that whatever you desire in your mate, you must be its reflection. I am very concerned about men and women in bad relationships who complain about their mates. It is as if they think there is some separation between themselves and the person who is causing them so much pain. When I hear women say that all men are dogs, and then I see them with a dog, that tells me a little about them. When I hear men say that sisters only want their money and they are involved with a materialistic sister, that is a reflection of their character. Brothers often say they have a problem with women who curse constantly, cannot cook, and like an abundance of sex. Often these women were dogged in a previous relationship because of these very things, yet their current man decided to ignore them.

I mentioned earlier that often we stay in relationships because there are voids in our own lives that relate back to our childhood. Many individuals stay in bad relationships because they honestly think that is all they deserve. Sometimes the pain is further expressed by questions such as, Where can I go, and who will want me? Remember that part of the science in selecting a mate is based on developing your self-esteem and attracting people to you that reinforce your self-esteem and value system. If your level of self-esteem is so low that you think you do not deserve better, or there is no one out there, you will believe it until you master the first African principle - man know thyself.

I believe part of the science of looking for a mate is to study yourself and then place yourself where people who think like you congregate. I think a major strength of Frances Welsing's theory of 28/30/2/4 is the notion that it may take each individual until the age of 28 to fully understand who you are, your values, aspirations and goals. Then and only then are you able to move to Karenga's second level of unity - family.

Over the years I have discovered five things about myself: I love the Lord, I am committed to the liberation struggle of African American people, I enjoy children, I enjoy playing sports and dancing. I learned that going to parties did not give me the opportunity to secure the evidence needed to find a mate. If I were single and looking for a mate I would attend church, a Black empowerment meeting and a PTA meeting or go to a park with children where I could meet other single parents. That is exactly what I did; I met my wife Rita at a church which offered activities that involved the Black experience and children.

When I tell people that it is important to place yourself where people who think like you congregate, invariably people write me hundreds of letters saying that they took my advice. They went to church for three weeks and are very upset with me because they have not found a mate. I am flabbergasted at this response because it is obvious they did not understand. If you love the Lord, you would have been in church anyway, and whether or not you found a mate would not be contingent on your returning. In addition, the good news is the Lord often works by providing a mate when you are not looking for one. You may simply be about His business at a Black liberation function or working with children. If you continue to do what you enjoy, your spirit and the aura that surrounds you will become so enticing that people will be attracted and gravitate to you without your knowledge, simply because they see the joy that you are experiencing.

I also believe it is imperative that we place more value on our lives, relationships and future stations in life. If you are preparing yourself to be a professor, politician, doctor, attorney or any other professional in life, it will take a certain type of mate to be married to you. How many of us have seriously looked at what we want out of life and the standard of living we want and then chose a mate that would complement our goals, aspirations and desired life-styles. Not everyone can be a pastor's husband or wife, a mayor's husband or wife or an actor's or actress' husband or wife. I am very blessed to be married to Rita. With the type of career I have that includes traveling four days a week and staying in the public eye, I needed to marry someone who was very secure and self-actualized. I often tease Rita because people in the public eye are often asked to represent their spouse, and this is the aspect that she tends to shy away from. My wife is very accomplished and manages our business very well, but she is not even remotely interested in being a public person. While I do not agree with Coretta Scott King's position in most areas, I think that both Coretta Scott King and Betty Shabazz have represented their husbands very well.

We live in a society that is stratified based on race, gender and class among other things. There was an article in a Black magazine that raised the question, Should Black women marry blue collar workers? The very fact this question was raised shows we are becoming more acculturated and class conscious. I often tell my audiences that many people who think they are part of the middle class are one paycheck away from poverty. If class is based on education, then what does that say about your mother or grandmother who did not have the degree but who scrubbed floors for you to secure yours? Historically, Black women were often educated and were able to become teachers while their men were working in factories or on the railroad. This is now viewed as "marrying down," or in sociology, endogamy. When women or men marry someone equal to or above them in terms of class stratification, this is called homogamy.

Earlier we mentioned that with the male shortage, sisters cannot take the position that they can only marry someone with an equal educational background. This is particularly true on a college campus where there are 700,000 African American females to only 517,000 African American males (with even fewer actually graduating). I do not see any contradiction with advocating that we need to find people who are complementary to us and our desired goals while at the same time avoiding class consciousness. This is the same dilemma that I often see in role model programs. Many of us have bought into a middle-class value system and think role models only come in the form of BA's and BMW's. I know of a great many brothers who have BA's and BMW's who are involved with several women, snort coke, and constantly break commitments. I also know a lot of brothers with high school diplomas, who wear overalls and white socks, drive a bus or a train, yet are very good role models because they are consistent and care about young people. We could reduce part of the problem between African American men and women by not allowing European values to divide us based on class.

Many brothers often tell me that they are a little disappointed that most of the women they meet provide them with an opportunity for a ready–made family. In God's ideal order, marriage comes before children. Many of us have reversed the process by having babies before marriage or getting divorced after our children were born, so there is no longer the opportunity to date as single adults with no additional responsibilities from children or former spouses. One brother told me that he was not against children, but he simply wanted to find one or two sisters to date where children were not part of the equation. When I share this with sisters, they become concerned about the fact that brothers think the children only belong to the mother and every brother who is complaining should also acknowledge that they have produced some of their own. For the record, I'd also like to acknowledge that I know several brothers who made the previous statement that have not made a baby.

I would like for the readers to now list on a sheet of paper all of the desires and traits they would like to see in their mates. Some people in my workshops tell me they need another sheet of paper because their list of characteristics is so long. I then ask the participants to write down beside each trait what they would have to be about in order to bring them to fruition. Often people erase some of their traits or characteristics. Remember, like attracts like. You reap what you sow! Remember, only God can change your mate. Many of us marry a vision of what we want rather than loving the person we have.

The last item we want to address in this chapter is that in the selection process, one of the things we need to be concerned with is the games that are often played in dating. Many brothers have a disguise called "Mr. Patient" and their sole objective is to have sex with the sister. They know better than showing their trump card on the first date, so Mr. Patient will play games and make it appear as if he

100

is not interested in her sexually. This is a disguise because in reality all he is after is sex, but he plays the game to deceive the sister into thinking that is not his intention. Remember, Mr. Patient cannot play this game by himself. Ms. You've-got-to-earn-it will play the game that no one will be involved with her sexually on the first date. The second or third dates are possibilities based on how much money is spent on her.

In addition to this, the last dynamic is the question of exclusivity. I personally believe that teenagers do not need to be involved in exclusive relationships; but in a world based on capitalism and ownership, it is understandable why this occurs. We mentioned earlier that often when the question of exclusivity is asked (usually prematurely) the brother or sister often does not give the response the partner wants to hear. If we understand that the major objective in this chapter is selecting a mate, it may be better to find the evidence by looking in several sources versus burying your head in the sand in one location.

Let's now turn to the chapter on values and observe how values affect everything that we do, including how we relate to each other.

Until you understand white supremacy
everything else will confuse you.

Chapter VI

Hip-Hop vs. MAAT (Values)

The title of this chapter is also the title of one of my earlier books. I take the fundamental position that relationships are based on values. The words that we use and our actions and behavior cannot be separated from our value system. A Hip-Hop value system is based on individualism, materialism, self-gratification and immediate and short-term gratification. This value system will drive people in a different way than the MAATIAN value system which is based on truth, justice, order, righteousness, harmony, balance and reciprocity. This entire chapter could be devoted to just one word: love, an overused and misunderstood word. Some people say they are falling in love, making love, being in love or even falling out of love. From an African value system, if the word love is used correctly, we cannot be in love on Thursday and fall out of love with that same person on Friday, unless the word was misunderstood. Ra Amen suggests that an appropriate synonym for the word love is selflessness. He goes further to state:

If the essence of love for example is giving selflessly or sacrificing for others, how can it then be equated with something that you can fall into or out of. Having spotted the discrepancy between selflessness and the

103

self-interest that accompanies most cases of falling in love, are you now ready to give up this mode of behavior?[1]

There is a difference between selflessness and self–interest that is associated with the values of falling in and out of love with someone. In an African value system, if I love you, it is not based on what you do for me, but more on what I can do for you. This concept is so distant from European values because in order to love someone based on their needs not yours requires a negotiation. Many couples are heard saying, "If you do this for me then I will do that for you." This is not love, it is a contract. In an African value system, the principles of MAAT: balance, harmony and reciprocity, are freely given without negotiations and contracts.

When comments are made such as women give sex for love and men give love for sex, the conflict here is that individuals are operating on different values. In Terry McMillan's bestseller *Waiting to Exhale*, the character Savannah had an excellent weekend and thought that by giving sex she would receive love afterwards. She dealt with the brother from her value system, but did not understand that some men give love for sex. The compassion and understanding she was receiving, which she thought was love, was actually a smoke screen so he could get what he really wanted -- sex.

In the value system of the West, men and women have a different view of their bodies and sexual relations. Many women will stay in a bad relationship if they have become sexually involved with the person because they believe the sexual act creates a bond with their partner. The problem arises when the other partner does not bring the same level of commitment to the bedroom. To that person it was

104

just a sexual act that can be consummated before marriage and outside of marriage and is not as meaningful. Unfortunately, more and more women are beginning to adopt the value system of men and look at sex as merely a sexual act rather than an expression of commitment that only takes place within the context of marriage. In a traditional Eastern spiritual value system, marriage preceded the sexual act and both male and female brought to the sexual act the same reverence.

There is no separation between words, behaviors and values when men describe the act of sex using the "f" word, the "b" word or other expressions such as ram, screw, bam, jam or f_ _ _. When some rappers describe in very misogynistic terms their view of women, they are clearly expressing their values.

Maulana Karenga says that from a values perspective, some of us are in connections and others of us are in relationships. Karenga writes:

> The capitalists, racists and sexist characters of this country argue for and encourage connections not quality relationships: superficial, utilitarian, alienated and short-term. The average Black man sees and treats the Black woman as he is seen and treated and he sees other women treated - as a commodity, a slave servant, a sexual and social utility. He duplicates the relationship of a ruler - ruled oppressor - oppressed exploiter - exploited. Blinded and deadened by his own deformation and denial on a societal level the average Black man seeks satisfaction on a personal level by imposing the same deformation and denial on his woman.[2]

Karenga goes on to outline that there are four major connections which include: cash, flesh, force and dependency. Connections are seen in dichotomous relationships and are

105

based on power, selfishness, greed and exploitation.

The bottom line for most individuals in connections is what they can get out of them. In a relationship that is based on the principle of MAAT, i.e. harmony, balance and reciprocity, love is freely given. Kalamu Ya Salaam says, Hofu ni Kwenu, my fear is for you. Can you imagine a world where you no longer have to watch your back and worry about Darwin's theory of self preservation? All you would have to do is try to make the world better for someone else without having to worry about your own interests. This is so far from the Hip-Hop, New Jack value system that for many of us it is unimaginable.

Let me briefly describe the two most frequent connections in America: the cash connection and the flesh connection. In *Hip-Hop vs. MAAT*, one of the vignettes we used described the cash connection in which men view women as objects that can be purchased. If I spend a certain amount of money on you on a given evening, then you owe me. The following is an example of how this is expressed.

It was four o'clock in the afternoon. Just one more hour and Raynard would be off work. He was already beginning to plan this big evening and anticipating how things were going to go between himself and Carolyn. He would start the evening off by picking her up and giving her a dozen roses. He was then going to take her to dinner. Raynard still could not determine whether the ambiance was better than the meal or vice-versa because they were both five star. This would precede a play. He was very confident that roses, dinner, a play and good conversation would give him what he truly wanted and from his perspective rightfully deserved - her body. In another downtown office Carolyn had her own plans for the evening. She had already decided to wear her "killer dress." The dress did one of two things. It either made men turn their heads when she walked by or it made their mouths come open because it was that kind of outfit. Carolyn also knew she had the perfect figure to complement this dress. She knew the combination of this dress and her body would be too much for Raynard to handle. She had already decided that if Raynard acted right tonight that she would give him her "garden." Ohhh, for sure, he was going to have to earn it. She had already decided that in order to get "this" there would have to be some flowers, and dinner would have to be at a very exquisite restaurant. The play could be mediocre as long as there was good conversation dispersed throughout the evening. After the flowers, dinner, play and conversation, Raynard took her home. They got undressed and she looked into his eyes and said, "I give it all to you." He returned the look and said, "I love you." That was Friday night. It's now Monday morning and Carolyn is in her office wondering why she has not heard from Raynard. Could it be that some men give love for sex while some women give sex for love?[3]

The above vignette shows both the cash and flesh connection. In a capitalistic society, everything is reduced to a commodity that can be purchased. Men, women and their bodies can be owned, sold and exchanged. It is no accident that in a material economy and a value system based on power relationships, prostitution and pornography continue to flourish.

Earlier in the book we indicated that if a male dates throughout his life it will cost him approximately $70,000. As we saw in the previous vignette, because Raynard had spent $200 that night he thought Carolyn owed him. This not only illustrates cash but her body represents flesh.

It is a sad commentary that things we thought were given to us as gifts we will be asked to return if there is a breakup. This leads us to question whether it was ever really a gift or merely a loan

107

based upon the current conditions. If that connection were to dissolve, all "gifts" are expected to be returned. This is another indication of the values that we live with every day.

In America the average marriage or relationship lasts 18 months. This seems to be comparable with the capitalistic economy that reinforces Alvin Tolfler's book *Future Shock*, where we live in a throwaway society. After 15-18 months of being together, many of us tire of each other and throw each other away and enter the marketplace to find somebody new.

US News & World Report predicts that in the year 2033, relationships will be a confusing tangle as a result of people living longer and changing mates to suit the seasons of their lives. The editors go on to predict that the growing trend of serial marriages will be a normal and planned part of adulthood.[4]

At the outset of the book we quoted Neely Fuller who says, "Until you understand White supremacy everything else will confuse you." Until this occurs, African American people will have a Eurocentric, capitalistic and sexist view of their mates. As Fanon wrote in *Black Skin, White Masks*, we look Black but our value system reflects a Eurocentric worldview. Some African American women expect African American men to be the major breadwinners. Some African American men will not understand that they are not in control of the means of production and cannot determine whether their plant remains in Detroit or moves to Mexico. She will look at him the way White women look at their men, as commodities that are supposed to provide financial stability, a house with a two-car garage and a trip to Disney World once a year. If African American men do not understand White supremacy they will expect that they should be able to provide these things for their wives. They will also expect their women to be submissive and financially dependent on them because of the patriarchal society in which we live.

It is becoming increasingly difficult for African Americans to provide the financial, emotional and spiritual stability that marriage requires in a racist, sexist, class–conscious environment. In the classified ads, none of the applicants were seeking someone who understood their history, culture and White supremacy. Until we understand the significance of Neely Fuller's position then marital stability is a fleeting desire. Couples must understand the need to come together to defeat White supremacy.

Let's apply the issue of values, the Hip Hop vs. MAAT dichotomy, to four significant issues that are affecting relationships: control, jealousy, shacking and polygamy. We operate in a value system that promotes racism, classism, and sexism. It is based on insecurity, where people rationalize that differences make them superior. We look for differences rather than commonalities, we are diunital versus biunital. In most marriages there is a power struggle that is played out to determine who will be in control. Unfortunately, some advocate that the person who has the greatest commitment to the relationship has the least power in it.

In the following chapter on solutions we will talk about people who are now afraid to love again because they have been hurt. Many of these individuals state that they will never give themselves fully to anyone again. It is because of this fear of losing power that nice guys finish last as stated in the previous chapter on selecting a mate. To put all of your cards on the table and let someone know that you love them, need them and are committed to them, individuals run the risk of being controlled by that person. This does not have to happen if both parties share a MAAT and/or Nguzo Saba value system. In talking to people and reading the classified ads, an African frame of reference and value system is not mentioned or sought. Therefore we attempt, consciously or unconsciously, and to various degrees, to be African in an Eurocentric environment. Please note that even Europeans are having a difficult time staying married within their own value system.

In the chapter on marital issues we made reference to the concept of oppression and observed that many African American men are frustrated at not being able to become actualized in a world based on White male supremacy. These men feel the only aspect of their lives they can control is their women. Values are clearly expressed within the context of wife abuse and rape. Earlier I mentioned my wife, who says, "This is Rita." Translated this means Rita understands power and will not be a domestic victim. She can think for herself and will not sit idly while I beat the hell out of her.

Ideally, no one should want to control someone else, but as we have discovered with the issue of integration and desegregation (there is a difference between the two), people who have power are not going to respect you until you respect yourself. As Frederick Douglass said, "Power concedes nothing without a struggle." We live in a world of power relationships and it is imperative that people who are oppressed begin to understand the nature of the oppressor. They should develop a defense mechanism based on an African cosmology versus

110

Eurocentric acculturation. Let me be more succinct: wife abuse is rampant and women allow men to control them. Let us also understand that the issue here is not about replacing one group in power with another. The issue is not about control, rather about living in harmony and balance with one another. In most marriages the power struggle is played out in three major areas: money, time and sex.

The next factor is jealousy and its relationship to values. I will never forget Maulana Karenga's statement that in a materialistic society, we are more concerned about someone making love to our mate's body than making love to their mind. In a materialistic world, many of us are unconcerned about our mates being involved in a mentally or spiritually fulfilling conversation but are very concerned about someone being physically intimate with our mate. The whole issue of jealousy is tied to the capitalistic concept of ownership. "That's my man/woman, and you better not put your hands on him/her!" In an African value system, you cannot lose what you do not have, but you freely give your mate to the world with the expectation that the person will come back to you.

There are couples that spend an inordinate amount of time monitoring the whereabouts of their spouses. Can you imagine being married to or in a relationship with someone who would drive his mate to work, not out of concern or consideration, but for fear that someone may talk to her while taking public transportation? Can you imagine having your spouse monitored by a colleague on the job or assigning someone to patrol the area in the evening when you are not available? There are thousands of relationships where this investigative work has become the norm. The apex of the problem is best expressed when individuals (primarily women) want to leave the relationship because they have had enough. The other spouse expresses jealousy in such strong terms they threaten to kill their mate before they will allow the person to be with anyone else. What is it about Eurocentric values that an individual would resort to killing someone rather than allowing them to be with someone else? It reminds me of the sickness of a small minority in South Africa who take the position that they would blow the country up before sharing power and allowing democratic control by the majority. The unfortunate reality is that people who are powerless feel that the people who do have power are not playing fair. This is why Neely Fuller takes the position that until you understand White supremacy everything else will confuse you. Therefore all of us collectively, women in particular, need to be mindful of being in any relationship with someone who has jealous tendencies. These people are sick and consumed by Eurocentric value systems that are not healthy for them or the community. It is an oxymoron to say "I killed her because I loved her."

The next issue we want to explore from a Hip-Hop/MAAT perspective is shacking. In one of the anecdotes we gave at the beginning of the book, a brother raised the question, Why should we get married in the White man's court? She knows I love her. He went on to say that they needed to live together first and see how the relationship would work. This clearly expresses a value system where commitment does not exist because the couple is practicing or playing at marriage before trying the real thing. Studies indicate that relationships where couples are shacking are even shorter than marriages. While marriages boast of an average 18-month duration, couples who shack last only 9-12 months, primarily because commitment is not present.[5] Because of this lack of commitment, individuals are not willing to make the ultimate decision. They have acknowledged that the commitment is not there, but they want to play for a while and hope the commitment will come later. It is amazing how we can rationalize our behavior. I am sure some people feel there is some logic in not spending money in the White man's court to get married if they feel the relationship will end in divorce eventually and result in extensive legal fees. I have heard couples who have lived together for so long that the woman legally changed her name and when children were born, they all had the same last name. Insurance policies and wills are created with each person being the beneficiary to the other, all of this outside of the context of marriage. It is amazing how people go to such great lengths and are still unable to make the ultimate commitment of being together for the rest of their lives. This to me is a reflection of the fickle commodity value system of the West where new productions and new relationships change every six-to-twelve months.

Fundamentally, the issue is whether to shack or to marry, to operate with a commitment or hope that a commitment will eventually develop. You either are committed to your mate or you are not. If you are, you should be married. If you are not, you need to question if you need to even live together or simply date. For some sisters to naively believe that just because their man said "I'm going to marry you" seven years ago "but in the meantime let's shack" is absurd. In fact, that statement is an indication that something is missing. It is not only a values crisis but a reflection on the character of African American men who have not made a commitment to God, themselves or their race. Their lease, car note and credit cards are not in their names but in their girlfriend's or mother's names. They are unable to make a lifetime commitment to anyone or anything. Some "shackers" rationalize their decision due to the high divorce rate and the possibility of lifestyle incompatibility; they feel shacking will give them an opportunity to observe each other in a household setting. I would argue that if you court looking for evidence, specifically when you visit one another and are involved in a thorough premarital counseling session that will encompass this area, you will not need to shack.

The next issue we want to look at from a values perspective is polygamy. An entire book could be written on this subject. All of us have strong opinions about polygamy, and yet many of us have not dissected all the issues and acknowledged that our position has been developed from our cultural and religious orientation. I would not expect an African American female who is a Christian to have the same views as an African born in a traditional environment who is Muslim. The position of each individual is based on the value system in which they have lived. I have had the fortunate opportunity to be a Christian, study the Qu'ran, visit Africa and conduct in-depth interviews with men and women, and read hundreds of books on African history and male/female relationships in order to arrive at these conclusions:

1. Polygamy is better than unofficial sharing and

serial monogamy. It is ridiculous for people to tell me they are against polygamy while currently involved in an extramarital affair and not see the contradiction in their position. I mentioned in a prior chapter that 75 percent of all men and 50 percent of all women are involved in extramarital affairs, and the number is rising. Yet if we interviewed those people, 90 percent or more would say they are not in favor of polygamy.

2. Polygamy is only necessary when there is a male shortage. When I visited Ghana and interviewed numerous people, both young and old, on the issue of polygamy, I discovered it is almost nonexistent, particularly in the younger and Christian community. They all indicated that the male shortage is not a factor in Ghana, therefore they did not see a need for polygamy. They felt that some elders and Muslims were holding on to traditions that were no longer necessary. For the African American community to adopt polygamy in order to address the problem of the male shortage, we accept the permanence of that reality. I often ask brothers, What would be more effective, to be involved with two to three women or to become a member of a rites-of-passage or other empowering program or activity that will develop African American boys into men? Fundamentally, I want brothers to come clean and ask themselves if they are promoting polygamy out of concern for sisters or their own personal greed and aggrandizement?

3. I am concerned about people who attempt to mix cultures, and want to be African in America only in select cultural aspects. I have seen African Americans adopt polygamy, and the male in the

115

relationship does not work, and all parties are living on welfare. If we are going to adopt polygamy we need to understand that traditionally, the African male had to provide economic resources for each household. I am willing to acknowledge that living in America is expensive and that women can also work just as they would in a monogamous arrangement. Polygamy in America should not be practiced in instances where the male is not working, and everyone is living on welfare. I have seen situations where only the women worked. I think the most fundamental factor to the acceptance of polygamy in America is that in those parts of Africa where it has been or is presently in effect, the society groomed the children at inception to accept its virtue. It is very difficult for an American female from infancy to 21 to be taught to value monogamy only to be told at 21 that because of the male shortage she will have to share. In addition, polygamy was a response to the male shortage, and not only was it a concern of the larger community, elders and men, but it was also a concern to the women. For that reason the first woman would choose the second woman. Polygamy therefore was not designed to satisfy the African male and allow him to choose the woman of his choice. Polygamy was designed to ensure that all women were given an opportunity to procreate and have a family. This was so important that the first wife was concerned about her sisters. In America, I see brothers moving on to the second and third wife without the first having any knowledge.

4. To reinforce the third point, I believe that whatever decisions are to be made to address the male shortage must be made by women. If brothers

are making the decisions, we will never know if the decisions were made for personal interests or for the salvation of the race. Many sisters tell me they have reviewed their options (some of them mentioned in the chapter titled "Where are the Brothers?"), and most have not chosen polygamy to address the male shortage. Lastly, because I am a Christian, I look to my Lord and Savior for an answer. The scripture says:

> And God said for this reason a man will leave his father and mother and unite with his wife and the two will become one. *Matthew 19:5*

It does not say wives. The Bible is very clear on God's position. I would encourage you to read *African Origins of Western Religions* by Dr. Yosef ben Jochannan, *The Black Presence in the Bible* by Walter McCray, *Troubling Biblical Waters* and *Stony the Road We Trod* by Cain Felder and the eighth chapter of the book of Acts. For those wondering why an Africentrist believes in Christianity, bear in mind that it was not introduced to Africans in 1619 on slave ships, but this scripture shows an Ethiopian eunuch representing Candace in 32 B.C. was reading the book of Isaiah.

When I interviewed members of the Nation of Islam, they told me that because they are growing in Islam and because of the rigors of being a Black man in America they were not allowed to marry more than one woman. As much as I respect the work of Minister Louis Farrakhan and the Nation of Islam, I did not believe for a minute his 1993 Savior's Day presentation that Elijah Muhammad was practicing polygamy. If he was practicing polygamy why couldn't he tell his national representative Malcolm X? Why did two of his mistresses complain to Malcolm? Why was his estate tied in probate court among these women? The Holy Qu'ran states:

> And if you fear you can't act equitably towards women, then marry such women as seen good to you, two and three and four, but if you fear that you will not do justice, then marry only one.   Sura 4:3

It is very difficult to discuss in one chapter an issue as monumental and intangible as values. In the spirit of MAAT, let's contrast those virtues with the issues previously cited.

THE SEVEN PRINCIPLES OF MAAT	RELATIONSHIP ISSUES
Truth	Cheating
	Lying
Justice	
	Emotional and physical abuse
Righteousness	
	Jealousy
	Shacking
Order	
	Friendship
Harmony	Money management
	Control
Balance	
	Personal and sexual gratification
Reciprocity	Household chores

I would like for you to apply the seven cardinal

virtues of MAAT to the relationship issues. I want you to honestly assess where you are from a values perspective on these issues.

Can we lie and cheat on our mate and practice the principles of truth and righteousness? Can there be harmony with emotional and physical abuse? Can we believe in reciprocity and be jealous and not share household chores? Can there be order shacking the American way?

Ra Un Nefer Amen in his excellent book titled *An Afrocentric Guide to Spiritual Union* indicates that:

> The key element in the regulation of people's lives concerns the understanding of evil, which in reality is synonymous with the causes of problems in man's life. We will see that evil is intrinsically tied up with the animal portions of man's brain. Rather than being an entity it is misperceived or misconceptualized by Westerners. It is the product of allowing the animal faculties to lead our behavior. The Old Testament scholars, in writing about the fall of man understood that the serpent they borrowed from the Kemetic psychological literature was a hieroglyph for reality and the brain/soul of people. The Western world would have understood that the transaction that took place in the garden of Eden represented an event that goes on in every person each and every time a desire or emotional impulse attempts to lead the way. If you allow your likes to dictate what you eat, who you mate with, how you mate and so on, would you not most likely end up in trouble? An important aspect of African philosophy is the belief from empirical evidence that man's life precedes and survives beyond the existence of his physical body which is merely the tool that allows man experience in the physical realm. Man from the African perspective is essentially a spiritual being.[6]

Spiritual union is therefore a reflection of the ultimate order of nature. Our spirituality prevails over our physical desires as an indication that we are never entirely in control.

The Divisions of the Spirit

The seventh spiritual division, sometimes called Khab, is our physical body which develops in all of us and gives us the illusion that we are separate beings and that reality is broken into a time and space continuum. The sixth division is called Khaibit and is the source of emotions, sense perceptions, sensual phenomena, desires, pleasures, irritability, pain and is developed in everyone. The fifth division known as Sahu is man's lower intellectual faculties such as memory, imitation and imagination and is available in about half of the population. The fourth division, Ab, represents the ability to synthesize, perform abstract or cosmological thinking and the ability to look for unity and the interrelationship between all people and things. It is here in the fourth division that man is able to understand the principles of MAAT. This concept is not evolved in most persons, initiation is needed. The third division, Shekem, allows man to influence physical events through spiritual power. It is not evolved in most persons and initiation is needed. The second division, Khu, is the ability to arrive at perfect solutions to all problems. This is not evolved in most persons and initiation is needed. The highest division is Ba, the ability to unite all interests in society. At this point the spirit is beyond all likes and dislikes, it is the universal spirit, the world spirit. All creatures are integral parts of this body. It is not evolved in most persons and initiation is needed. The last three divisions of the spirit are fully independent of the brain.[7]

Please understand that in the above spiritual table, the higher functions control the lower ones. The higher the division we function from spiritually, the less evil there will be in our behavior. Unlike Western tradition which concentrates on pouring information into a person (education) in the belief that this will make a better person, African society is concentrated on the graduated awakening and development (initiation) of the higher divisions of the spirit. It cannot be overstated that education is merely an act of pouring information into one of the divisions of the lower spirit, fifth, sixth or seventh, while behavior control is the function of the four higher divisions.

I would like for you to pause and ask yourself where you are on this spiritual topology. Refer to the ten relationship issues we wanted you to apply to the seven cardinal virtues of MAAT and ask yourself, In what spiritual division is a person who belongs in any of these ten relationships issues?

As we conclude this chapter, let's return back to the fundamental principles of love. In the lower divisions, love rests on the premise that you make me feel good. However, in the higher divisions, love reflects that I am in harmony with you and $1+1=1$. It is because I love you that I give all of myself to you, because in giving myself to you, I give to myself. Life is circular, in harmony and in balance. There is no separation from my spirit and your spirit. This definition of love is so far removed from the Western world and its value system that it is very difficult to comprehend, particularly if you are operating in the last three divisions. Let's now look at our chapter on solutions, though I hope you have seen solutions throughout the book.

Successfully married couples give each other quality time.
Hugs should be given daily and couples should learn to play.

CHAPTER VII

SOLUTIONS

Throughout the book, we have been attempting to provide solutions to the myriad of problems that are affecting us in male/female relationships. Our major objective has been to address the issue that the official divorce rate is 50 percent and 80 percent unofficially, while in more traditional societies, specifically African, the divorce rate is five percent.

If the major problem for African people is White supremacy, the first solution needs to be gearing our union towards defeating the enemy of racism, capitalism and sexism. African people had greater marital stability in slave dungeons, on slave ships during the middle passage, on the plantation and through mass migrations Northward than we have as we near the twenty-first century. What was it about the African psyche that compelled a wife who was sold to North Carolina and a husband who was sold to Georgia to look for each other?

Today if the husband is offered a job in Seattle and the wife wants to stay in Detroit or vice versa, in many cases the couple will break up before they find a mutually satisfactory solution. Many African scholars propose that the reason we were able to stay together in the past was because we felt that family and marriage were important and something to be valued. Our ancestors felt that the family was the basic unit of the nation and the only way African people could survive was if the African family survived.

The staggering divorce rate makes it painfully obvious that our ancestor's commitment to their relationships does not exist in our relationships today. Couples should not marry until they confront the major marital issues that are causing divorce, which include: economics, self-esteem, sexual compatibility and infidelity, lack of communication, oppression, i.e., racism, sexism and classism, drug abuse, blended families, lifestyle incompatibility and in-laws. It is amazing how people know the divorce rate is fifty percent and walk down the aisle without seriously addressing the fact that these issues could affect them. Marital counselors and ministers should make sure that before they marry other couples, these issues are addressed.

I made reference in earlier chapters to Frances Welsing's theory 28/30/2/4. The theory states that couples should not marry until they have taken responsibility for their own happiness. Welsing suggests this may take until an individual reaches the age of 28. She then proposes waiting two years before children are conceived. This time will allow the opportunity to further understand each other, discuss child rearing, develop savings and possibly finish studies and/or travel together. Welsing then advocates only bringing into the world the number of children you can adequately care for, which for most would be no more than two. Finally, children need lap time, nurturance and breast feeding. Dr. Welsing recommends spacing your children at least four years apart.[1]

The next solution is having realistic expectations of marriage. One of the major reasons why our ancestors were able to survive and maintain marital stability is that they had realistic expectations. Research shows that our expectations of marriage are now twelve times higher than before. I mentioned earlier that we need to view marriage as diapers, dishes, homework and a little bit of romance. Ernestine Walker, in her book titled *Black Relationships: Mating and Marriage*, raises the question, Are you suitable for marriage? She then offers six questions people should answer before walking down the aisle.

1. Do you have a realistic perception of what marriage is and what it is not?
2. Do you have an adequate amount of self knowledge?
3. Are you emotionally healthy with the appropriate amount of self-esteem?
4. Are you willing to compromise?
5. Are you a fairly effective communicator?
6. Do you really want your marriage to last?[2]

If you cannot answer these questions in the affirmative, it is recommended that you wait and develop yourself before one of the most important decisions of your life is made.

The next solution requires that we ask ourselves what would it be like or what is it like being married to me? Many of us, if we are honest, would acknowledge that we would not be able to be married to ourselves. Many of us are very complex and have so many idiosyncrasies that it would be hard for us to satisfy ourselves.

I know that being married to me is a challenge. I travel three or four days a week and when I am home, I am involved in child rearing, interviews, writing, office administration and involvement with community projects. My hobbies include reading, watching and taping documentaries, sports and exercising. Many of these activities require degrees of solitude. In addition, I am sometimes moody, self-centered, not as generous as I need to be and I do not do my fair share of the housework. My wife would also add that I am tight with the money. So who would want to be married to somebody whom they see only half the week? In addition when that person is in town he occupies himself with solitary activities, and when together may be moody and selfish.

I would like for the reader to pause for a moment and write what it would be like to be married to you, and be as critical as I was of myself. I did not mention some of my positive attributes; I think some of us are more complimentary than critical. Take a moment and be very objective and describe what it would be like being married to you.

Rita and I have a joke that we would not have any problems if the other spouse simply did things my way. A lot of adults feel their way is the right way, but since most of us are not mind readers, we cannot always predict what "my way" entails. That is one of the major reasons why some married people want to be single. If they were single, they would not have to talk with their mate about money distribution, furniture arrangement, time management, child rearing and so many other issues that come up in day-to-day living. Many people truly believe that if marital issues were handled their way they would not have these problems. What some people have found is when they have married someone who is insecure and unempowered, who lacks self-esteem and who will acquiesce to their mate's every whim, this too becomes very unchallenging, unfulfilling and boring, because we find out that we do not want to be married to ourselves. We really do need to be in communion with a fully actualized person, someone who will say "This is Rita."

One of the major reasons for the tremendous disparity between the divorce rate in Western and Eastern societies is that in America, everyone is present for the wedding ceremony, but few are invited and choose to be involved in the reconciliation. In an African value system, the two individuals are not just married to each other, they are married to the larger community that sanctioned the wedding. In the American experience, everyone is invited to the ceremony, but only the two individuals have the right to decide if they will stay together. Often, when people have expressed an interest in reconciliation, it was thwarted.

In the last chapter, "What Does the Lord Have to Say?" we will mention the concept of the third party. This concept is significant because if only two people vote there is a possibility of a split decision, which could lead to dissolution. There will be issues throughout the course of a marriage or relationship where the two parties simply will not agree. If they cannot reconcile, they unfortunately dissolve. In an African value system, there is always a third party. This source could be the larger community, the council of elders, grandparents or other designated persons. In the last chapter we will look at the Lord being the third party. I believe that relationships are destined to fail if only two people are allowed to vote. In the Western value system of New Jack, Hip-Hop and rugged individualism, most adults do not want anyone to be involved in their relationship. This parallels how we raise children in singular, nuclear homes without input from the extended family. There is an African proverb that states "it takes a whole village to raise one child," and we might add that it also takes that same village to keep spouses together.

In an earlier chapter, "Selecting a Mate," I mentioned that historically and in traditional societies in Africa, the parents are involved in the selection process. If that is not acceptable, we should at least join a church that requires satisfactory completion of premarital counseling. I commend churches that not only provide these sessions, but refuse to marry couples without satisfactory completion. Unfortunately because of egos, some couples who receive this advice will find another church or go to the courthouse rather than accept the recommendation and work on their weaknesses.

When trials and tribulations come in a marriage, and they will, it is imperative that a third party be collectively designated to assist the couple. I strongly suggest that if problems need to be discussed outside of the marriage they should be shared with happily married couples. As we all know, misery loves company and the worst thing a spouse can do is talk to someone who is divorced or unhappily married when problems surface in the relationship. Those people more often than not will not give sound advice or steadfastness needed to weather the storm.

Rita and I have been blessed to have Val and Ethel Jordan, who conduct marriage enrichment workshops for our church, as third party godparents to our marriage. On a couple of occasions we conferred with them, and because of their strong commitment to each other for the past fifty years, they simply laughed off the minor problems that we had and said they had encountered similar experiences, but stayed together. They have given us confidence, advice and Christian tenacity. Had we gone elsewhere, to people who were divorced, who did not value marriage or who were not God fearing, we may not be together today or be as committed to each other.

It is also important that before you run to talk to someone else about a problem, you thoroughly review your motive. One of the anecdotes we gave at the beginning of the book asked, Do you want to be right or do you want to be married? Val Jordan asked me this the first year of our marriage after I shared with him a problem. We have to honestly assess if we want to choose people who will be cheerleaders or people who will give us constructive criticism. In addition to that, we need to realize that when we share a particular frustration with another person on any given day, they will not be present when we reconcile, nor do they love our mate. Therefore, many times they may hold a grudge for weeks although the couple has resolved the issue.

Nathan and Julia Hare recommend that we also develop brotherhoods, sisterhoods and Kupenda (the African word for love) groups. It is very important that brothers come together and begin to share their experiences with each other. Research shows that when brothers experience a problem, because of their macho attitude and the inability of many men to share their intimate pain and secrets with another brother, they share them with sisters. Unfortunately, many brothers, while in one relationship become involved with another sister in a "rebound" relationship, which is not the best healing therapy. The cleansing process should have been done with a brother, not a sister. I also believe that there is less chance of cheating on your mate if you have the opportunity to share your feelings with someone of the same gender. As we said in the chapter "Selecting a Mate," many people that we say are our friends are really potential lovers because we have not resolved the sexual question. Sharing your pain with someone of the opposite sex should be reserved for a platonic relationship.

When I am in the locker room at the health club or at the barber shop and some brothers brag about their latest score with a sister or the number of babies they have produced, I feel it is my responsibility to share with them my Christocentric and Africenric values to see if I can upgrade the discussion to one of responsibility. Brotherhoods should begin to hold males accountable by emphasizing quality over quantity, and focusing on the best interests of women and children.

One of the major reasons why we recommend separate brotherhood and sisterhood groups is we have found that over the years in male/female relationship discussions, we put on airs when the opposite sex is present. We need to be forthright and honest with each other. Sisters need to respect each other's relationships, unless they agree to share a man. After we have developed brotherhood and sisterhood groups, then and only then are we able to come together in co-ed and Kupenda love groups. Kupenda should not be male and female bashing sessions, but rather an opportunity for constructive criticism and collective growth.

One of the major problems in male/female relationships that has been cited throughout the book is the issue of communication. Not only do we say things we should not have said, but often we do not listen. To listen is a verb, an active process. Joy Jones calls it listening with the Third Ear. Unfortunately, it has been said that women listen better than men. Women listen not only to what is said, but the emotion and feeling surrounding the statement. Sometimes I tease my audience by reminding them that often when we think we are listening to someone, we are actually thinking about what we are going to say next. It is impossible for someone to finish their thought and for you to immediately respond. There should be some pause, if only for a second, before you answer, if indeed you were actively listening. This is why many marital counselors in order to ensure people are listening ask participants to clearly state what the problem is without indicting the other individual, only the behavior. Then they ask each person to repeat what they heard the other person say to ensure that what was said is understood.

What happens when you win an argument? Does your spouse lose? If so, you also lose. Always remember that underneath anger is hurt and underneath hurt is love. John Powell, in the excellent book *The Secrets of Staying in Love*, talks about communication in a unique way. He says that many of us talk from the mouth rather than from the heart. Unfortunately, we play games with each other because we do not trust our mate with our heart. When a sister tells a brother to pack his bags and leave, what she really means underneath the hurt is I need you tonight, and I want to be with you. Rather than expressing what she really felt from her heart, she decided to speak from the mouth. The reason this happens is because, as mentioned earlier, the person who has the greatest commitment to the relationship has the least amount of power. Many of us do not want to appear powerless or vulnerable to our mates, therefore we protect our hearts with our mouths by saying things we do not mean. Robert Staples, in his book *The World of Black Singles*, agrees that vulnerability affects communication in relationships.

> Whenever there is an objective conflict, it is the most committed partner who generally gives in. Due to the black male's desire to maintain control of his situation, and his image of masculinity, refusal to make a commitment is one way of achieving the power balance in a relationship. As his emotional involvement with a woman increases, his feelings of insecurity may be heightened.[3]

The question I want to raise is, Why would you stay with someone if you could not trust them with your heart? If you are assuming that if they knew how you really felt they would exploit the opportunity, why do you stay?

I have been somewhat critical of myself throughout this book but I will acknowledge that one of my major strengths is my communication skills. Rita knows exactly how I feel and vice versa. I am able to meet people and remove the facade without game playing. I want to know your very essence, and it should be reciprocal.

Another excellent book in the area of relationship communication is *The Five Languages of Love* by Gary Chapman. The languages include words of affirmation, quality time, giving gift, acts of service and physical touch. Often in marriage the way we want to express love to our mate is not in their "language." You may buy your mate gifts because that is your language preference, but your mate may want affection expressed with quality time.

132

The net effect is speaking German to a French speaking spouse. I would like for you to list the five languages in your order of preference. Secondly, list your mate's language preferences. Have your mate do the same and then compare and share your findings.

A major reason for divorce is that couples seldom communicate in the same language. To be successful we must learn and speak the desired language of our mate. Note I emphasized the word speak; the first step is to learn, but many self-centered and stubborn spouses may know their mates' preference, but choose not to communicate in their mates' language because they desire to communicate in their own language.

Another important dimension in the communication arena is staying with the issue. I am a former debater and as a public speaker, I know that when I am asked a question I need to focus directly on the question and answer it accordingly. Unfortunately, in male/female relationships one individual may want to discuss a problem that took place tonight while the other person, knowing they were wrong tonight wants to discuss what went wrong over the past three years. My problem with this scenario is that nothing will be resolved by attempting to discuss tonight's problem along with other historical problems. I believe it is a much better discussion if the conversation is one dimensional.

Two words that are very hard for adults to say are "I'm sorry." Somehow even when we want to apologize, we do it in such a nebulous way that you never actually hear those two words. Often "I'm sorry" sounds like this: "I really didn't mean to do that, but you made me act this way." I guess this person is sorry, but by qualifying their apology with what you made them do makes you wonder if they really are sorry.

One of our ministers, Rev. Daniels, gave a superb sermon in which she mentioned that she was tired of people saying "I'm sorry;" she wanted to see the proof in their changed behavior.

When brothers tell sisters "I didn't mean to beat you last night," "I'm sorry for having an affair," or "I'm sorry for spending the money on cocaine" repeatedly, their ability to say the words is no longer the issue. We must demand, expect and see changed behavior. Saying "I'm sorry" should be taking an active step towards not repeating the unapproved of behavior. Take a moment and reflect on your praise/criticism ratio. Most of us criticize more than we praise. Try this week to compliment your mate more frequently and you'll be pleasantly surprised to see a change in their demeanor.

I asked my aunt before she died what was her secret for almost fifty years of marriage. She responded that she never believed Teddy Pendergrass or anyone else who believed in 50/50 and 60\40 relationship. She said her secret for marriage was to give 110 percent. She was not in a negotiation; she was in a marriage that was based on giving everything, not fractions or percentages. She also said that if the relationship dissolved, she would be sure that it was not the result of her negligence.

Research indicates that successfully married people give each other quality time. Some reports illustrate successful marriages receive at least 15 hours a week of qualitative communication. This figure increases to 30 hours if the couple is experiencing marital problems. If the assumption is that a marriage needs 15 hours a week or two hours a day of quality interaction, it would only make sense that this figure would increase if there are marital problems. Hugs should be given daily and we should learn to play together. I also suggest that if or when things become tense, reflect on the best five moments you have had with your mate and attempt to recreate the experience. Too many therapy sessions attempt to dissect problems rather than identify enjoyable marital moments and discuss opportunities to enjoy them again.

Another solution comes from the excellent book written by Ken Keyes entitled *A Conscious Person's Guide to Relationships*. In the book the author uses two very significant terms, addictions and preferences, just as in drug use. Addictions are those things that we have to have because we cannot function without them, while preferences are items you would like to have, but life can exist without them. Keyes takes the position that we all need to do inventory on ourselves and list our addictions. He points out the more addictions you possess, the more volatile your relationships. Keyes feels that when we break up or have an argument with our mate, our addictions are the culprits.

The following is an example of how this surfaces in relationships. A couple was supposed to meet for dinner at 7:30. The woman arrives at the restaurant at 7:15, the man is not there but this is not a problem because she is 15 minutes early. Seven thirty comes and still he has not arrived, but the woman is not worried because he is not late yet; by 7:45, he still has not shown up; 8:00 and 8:15 pass before he arrives at 8:30. The woman has a choice of either discussing why he was late and developing strategies on how to avoid his being late in the future and proceeding to enjoy the rest of the evening, or she can say that he made her mad because he was late. This last statement creates so much friction that they leave at 8:45, and are both upset for the rest of the week; they may even choose to discontinue the relationship.

The next scenario involves a married couple who are in bed at 10:00 p.m. Some males view sex like water - an addiction. This couple has been married for over ten years and have three children. The wife says "Baby, you know I love you. I've loved you for the past ten years, and I'm the mother of your children and I was up with one of them at 5:30 this morning. Can we do this tomorrow, next week, but please not tonight?" The husband has a choice of either complying, getting up and watching television, or he can say that she made him angry.

Unfortunately, many of us believe the addictions and problems in our relationships are with the other person and we think by changing personnel, we will eliminate the addiction; the sister with the issue of timeliness and the brother with the issue of sex will discover that in a new relationship their addiction will reappear. The sooner we realize that the addictions are ours and not our mates, the greater stability we will have in our relationships.

Please note the objective is not the elimination of all addictions. For example, a sister who has an addiction that she will not allow anyone to hit her, and is willing to sacrifice the relationship if this occurs, is correct. This addiction is healthy and demands respect from all parties. The major point that Ken Keyes wants to establish is that addictions are costly, and many of us have an inordinate amount.

Another solution that I have shared in some of my earlier writing is the Keisha/Kathy theory and the Eddie/Willie theory which address the issue of self-esteem. I believe that men know who to beat and who not to, and that men are not going to respect women until women respect themselves. Keisha feels very good about herself. She would like to have a man, but it is not mandatory. The sun will still shine and God will still be first in her life. Keisha is alive, growing and developing. On the other hand, Kathy does not feel complete without a man. She is emotionally and physically abused by her man. Kathy accepts whatever time he spends with her. I believe we have more Kathys than we are willing to admit. Having two sons in my household, girls call my sons all night long, and my wife and I literally have to make our sons get off the phone and return their phone calls at a later date, and more reasonable time. I also believe that the Keishas of the world do not backstab nor gossip, and they attempt to build unity among their sisters.

The skills that women need to administrate a school, run a business or supervise a program are not the same skills needed to be happily married. While attending Morgan State, an elder told me "there is nothing like a North Carolina woman." I wanted him to elaborate, and he, like Joy Jones, said that this particular type of woman is one that is academically competent, has achieved in the outside world, but is able to make her man feel like a man when she returns home. Valerie Shaw, in the book titled *Himpressions*, elaborates:

> There is no telling how far you can throw a little subtlety. Subtlety is what brothers see in Southern girls. They know how to take an idea and make a man claim it as his own. The same goes for Asian women, and yes White women. I've seen White women work their mojo's on our brothers without so much as working up a sweat. For many of them pampering the Black man is as easy as putting on a pair of pantyhose. While many sisters are throwing out evil looks and

137

wild words to get what they want, ladies of other cultures are getting mileage out of a smile, a little encouragement, approval, recognition, a kiss hello or a kiss goodbye. There is no telling how far a little kindness will go with our brothers. If you have a problem giving anything more than a brother requires, watch how some women can get an open line of credit in the bank of love while other women have to pay to play and pay interest besides.[4]

Valerie Shaw goes on to provide 101 ways to pamper your Black man. Listed below are a few:

- Take his mother to lunch.
- Listen to him.
- Want the best for him.
- Watch TV with him.
- Ask him to teach you something and take a real interest in learning it.
- Learn to be a good cook.
- Limit your time on the telephone.
- Treat his ex-wife, the mother of his children, with respect.
- Spend time with his kids.
- Even after you have won his heart, flirt with him.
- Pray for him and with him.[5]

In Joy Jones book, *Between Black Women,* she reflected on her high school reunion and mentioned that relationships are like dancing. She knew the dance, but acknowledged that both the man and woman could not lead, someone has to follow. Following does not make anyone less of a person because in dancing just as in relationships we have to be able to move with each other.[6]

It's amazing with the male shortage how some women have received numerous marital proposals.

I interviewed several women who collectively have had over 20 proposals and found these women appreciated male interests, i.e., they understood and played sports, were great listeners and had that North Carolina persona of being career-oriented while at the same time being feminine and providing a comfortable home.

The other example is the Eddie/Willie theory. Willie makes babies, while Eddie takes care of them. Willie will only do work outside of the house because he believes man's work is on the outside, and woman's work is on the inside. Eddie will do whatever it takes inside or out, especially if schedules are different and work needs to be done. Willie does not attend church, and discourages his wife from going; Eddie not only encourages his wife to go to church but he also goes with her.

Pause for a moment and ask yourself, do you act like Keisha or Kathy? Eddie or Willie?

The next solutions come from a book titled *The Dance Away Lover*. In this book, Daniel Goldstein points out that there are three stages in a relationship. Phase one is the romantic stage or the feel good stage. I have always been a strong admirer of Smokey Robinson, and between Smokey, Anita, Luther and Sade, stage one can feel so good; you can almost imagine running through grassy fields and never touching the ground. The romantic stage is enjoyable because it requires nothing from us but feeling and looking good. Most of us in the romantic stage try to impress one another. Many people feel this stage lasts three to four months. The book describes stage two as the problem stage. The person that made you feel so wonderful in stage one is now on your last nerve. Many of us spend our entire lives vacillating between stage one and stage two; when we experience the problems of stage two we think the solution is finding another mate with whom we can experience the joy of stage one again. Stage three is the commitment stage. This stage requires work that Smokey, Anita, Luther and Sade cannot provide. This stage enables you to look your mate in the eye and say, "I know we are going to have problems, but I would have problems no matter who I was with, so I might as well stay in this relationship and work them out in order to reach a commitment." Oftentimes, a disgruntled spouse will complain and say, "I'm not getting what I want out of the marriage." We all must understand we did not enter marriage solely for our own appeasement. We also vowed to do something for our partner. Marriage is not a bargain to be bartered, negotiated, sold and returned. It is a lifetime covenant with you and the Lord where divorce is not an option.

In the book *Divorce Busting*, Michele Weiner-Davis challenges us to stay together. She mentions that divorce does not solve problems, but only creates a new set.

There are very few of us who reach stage three. I am happy to admit that I have reached this stage in my marriage. I said I would not write this book on relationships until I had. Again I want you to pause and ask yourself what stage are you in? The romantic, problem or commitment stage? When I ask my audiences this question some people respond by asking what if you are not in a relationship at all? This is why we included the chapters "Where are the Brothers?" and "Selecting a Mate." Many of us are not in the romantic stage, and for that reason the solution chapter is not the last chapter in this book. For those who are not in stage

140

one, two or three or are having problems in those various stages, there remains some additional good news in the last chapter.

I want to close this chapter with the poem from Kahlil Gibran called "Joy and Sorrow." Frankie Beverly and Maze changed the song for rhyming purposes calling it "Joy and Pain." There are many of us who have said that because of the pain that we have experienced we would never love again. Unfortunately, we did not realize that the same person that could make us feel so good is the same person that could make us feel so bad. Kahlil writes:

Then a woman said speak to us of joy and sorrow and he answered your joy is your sorrow unmasked and the selfsame well from whence your laughter rises will often times fill with your tears. And how else can it be? The deeper the sallow carves into your being the more joy you will contain. Did not the cup that hold your wine the very cup that was burned in the powered oven? And did not the loot that soothes your spirit the very wood that was hollowed with knives? When you are joyous, look deep into your heart and you shall find it is only that which is giving you sorrow that is giving you joy. When you are sorrowful look again into your heart and you shall see that in truth you are weeping for that which has been your delight. Some of you say joy is greater that sorrow, and others say nay sorrow is the greatest. But I say unto you they are inseparable together they come, and when one sits alone with you at your board remember the other is asleep upon your bed. Verily you are suspended like scale between your sorrow and your joy. Only when you are empty are you at a standstill in balance. When the treasure keeper lifts you to where his gold and silver, needs must your joy or sorrow rise or fall.[7]

Husbands and wives would have a much easier time submitting to one another if they would first submit themselves to Christ.

CHAPTER VIII

WHAT DOES THE LORD HAVE TO SAY?

The divorce rate in the secular world is about 50 percent, but in the religious community, this figure is 1 out of 244 if couples pray, read and apply scripture and attend church together. When prayer was taken out of the public schools in 1962, the following year there was a marked increase in divorce. There really is power in prayer.[1]

It is suicidal for couples to think they can live within a morally decadent value system with a divorce rate of 50 percent and believe their romantic, sex-oriented, self-gratifying culture will suffice. Satan hates family, especially those who are believers. This reduced divorce rate shows Satan's job is more difficult among believers.

Individuals in marriages, like alcoholics, are powerless without God. They both operate without any power against affairs, pornography, loneliness, sexually suggestive videos and music, peer pressure and divorce in addition to all of Satan's other evil indulgences. The twelve basic principles of Alcoholics Anonymous can also be applied to relationships. They are:

1. We admitted we were powerless over our relationships - that our lives had become unmanageable.
2. We came to believe that a power greater than ourselves could restore us to sanity.
3. We made a decision to turn our will and our relationships over to the care of God, as we understand God.
4. We made a fearless and searching moral inventory of ourselves.
5. We confessed to God, to ourselves, and to our partners the exact nature of our wrongs.
6. We are entirely ready to have God remove all our defects of character.
7. We humbly asked God to forgive our shortcomings and to remove them.
8. We made a list of persons we had harmed, our mates in particular, and became willing to make amends to them all.
9. We made direct amends to such people wherever possible, except when to do so would injure them or others.
10. We continued to take personal inventory, and when we were wrong promptly admitted it.
11. We sought through prayer and meditation to improve our conscious contact with God as we understand God, praying only for knowledge of God's will for us and the power to carry that out.
12. Having had a spiritual awakening as a result of these steps, we tried to carry this message to others and to practice these principles in all our affairs.[2]

Throughout this chapter we must look to the Lord for direction. It was mentioned earlier that loneliness and being alone are not synonymous. In the present climate of male shortages and the trials of staying together, we must ask the Lord what are the benefits of remaining single.

> Actually I would prefer that all of you were as I am but each one has a special gift from God, one person this gift another one that gift. Now to the unmarried and to the widows I say that it would be better for you to continue to live alone as I do. But I would rather spare you the everyday trouble that married people will have. I would like you to be free from worry. An unmarried man concerns himself with the Lord's work because he is trying to please the Lord. But a married man concerns himself with worldly matters, because he wants to please his wife. And so he is pulled in two directions. An unmarried woman or virgin concerns herself with the Lord's work because she wants to be dedicated both in body and in spirit; for a married woman concerns herself with worldly matters because she wants to please her husband.
>
> *I Corinthians 7:7-8, 28, 32-34*

Further, we must realize that the Lord already has a plan for helping us to find a mate. The Lord knows that everyone longs to give themselves completely to someone, to have a deep soul relationship with another and to be loved thoroughly and exclusively. God says that not until you are satisfied, fulfilled, content with living and being loved by Him alone will you be able to be united with another. You must be able to give yourself totally and unreservedly to God alone. God loves you for you are His child, but until you discover that only in Him is your satisfaction to be found you will not be able to accept and appreciate the perfect human relationship that He has planned for you. You will never be united with another, until you are united with Him.

In the chapter on selecting a mate, many suggestions were offered. The Lord has the following advice for one of the most important decisions of your life.

Be not unequally yoked together with unbelievers: but with fellowship hath righteousness with unrighteousness and with communion hath light with darkness. How can right and wrong be partners? How can light and darkness live together?

II Corinthians 6:14

If a Christian man has a wife who is an unbeliever and she agrees to go on living with him he must not divorce her. And if a Christian woman is married to a man who is an unbeliever and he agrees to go on living with her she must not divorce him. For the unbelieving husband is made acceptable to God by being united to his wife. And the unbelieving wife is made acceptable to God by being united to a Christian husband. However if the one who is not a believer wishes to leave the Christian partner let it be so. In such cases the Christian partner or the husband or wife is free to act. God has called you to live in peace. How can you be sure Christian wife that you will not save your husband or how can you be sure Christian husband that you will not save your wife.

I Corinthians 7:12-16

The alarming statistics involving teen sexuality, pregnancy, conception out-of-wedlock, infidelity and sexually transmitted diseases is a clarion call that humans need help in their sexual affairs. The Bible teaches:

You know that your bodies are parts of the body of Christ. Shall I take a part of Christ's body and make it a part of the body of a prostitute? Impossible! Or perhaps you do not know that the man who joins his body to a prostitute's becomes physically one with her? The scripture says quite plainly the two will become one body but he who joins himself to the Lord becomes spiritually one with Him. Avoid immorality. Any other sin a man commits does not affect his body but the man who is guilty of sexual immorality sins against his own body.

I Corinthians 6:15-18

146

In the ideal world where serving God is primary, and an adequate ratio of men to women exists, the Lord prefers for men and women to be together.

> Then the Lord said it is not good for man to live alone I will make a suitable companion to help him. That is why a man leaves his father and mother and is united with his wife and they become one.
> *Genesis 2:18,21*

Our primary concern throughout this book has been the reduction, if not the elimination, of divorce. The Lord is very clear on this issue.

> Man must not separate then, what God has joined together. *Mark 10:9*

> But now I tell you: if a man divorces his wife for any cause other than her unfaithfulness then he is guilty of making her commit adultery if she marries again. And the man who marries her commits adultery also.
> *Matthew 5:32*

> I hate divorce says the Lord God of Israel. I hate it when one of you does such a cruel thing to his wife. Make sure that you do not break your promise to be faithful to your wife. *Malachi 2:16*

There is probably no scripture in the Bible that is more misunderstood and taken advantage of than Ephesians 5:21-28. There are brothers who are not in the church, not in Christ and have never read the word, but somehow through osmosis know this particular scripture, specifically verse 24 where it states wives must submit themselves completely to their husbands.

> Submit yourselves to one another because of your reverence for Christ. Wives, submit yourselves to your husbands as to the Lord for a husband has authority

over his wife just has Christ has authority over the church. And Christ is himself the savior of the church his body. And so wives must submit themselves completely to their husbands just as the church submits itself to Christ. Husbands, love your wives just as Christ loved the church and gave his life for it. Men ought to love their wives just as they love their own bodies. A man who loves his wife loves himself.

Ephesians 5: 21-28

Scripture should always be read in context by reading the verses before and after to derive a better understanding. If brothers had read verse 21, they would have discovered that both husband and wife were to submit to one another as they simultaneously submit themselves to Christ. I believe that African American women would have no problem submitting themselves to their husbands if they knew that before he made any decision he would submit himself to Christ. Brothers cannot have it both ways. If they want their wives to submit to them; it is imperative that they submit themselves to Christ.

The scripture is also sensitive because of its sexist language. The Bible is filled with the pronoun He in reference to God and instructions to His people. In I Corinthians, Paul says women should be silent in the church. Some men use this scripture the same way some Whites used Ephesians 6:5 to say that slaves should obey their masters. Consequently, some Whites used this to rationalize slavery just as some men use I Corinthians to rationalize that women cannot be ministers in the church. Unfortunately, some of those ministers have not read Galatians 3:28, chapter 16 of Romans or the life of Deborah who was both a prophet and a judge.

Turning back to Ephesians 5, the most sensitive word is submit, or in some translations, obey. I think we can remove the sensitivity if we understand that verse 21 is the most important scripture. In this scripture both husband and wife have to submit to and obey each other as they submit to and obey Christ. I feel any serious brother reading Ephesians 5 in its entirety may decide it's too awesome a responsibility. Without the power of God, men are unable to love their wives the way Christ loved the church. In a Eurocentric value system, a leader, i.e., a dictator, is someone who is in control or maintains power over someone else. This concept is vastly different from an Africentric leader who is viewed as a healer or a servant, someone who lives by the example "the first shall be last and the last shall be first." Within this context, the man is more concerned that his wife and children have food before he eats. This is in contrast to the male eating all that he wants, and anything left over is given to his wife and children.

For a wife to submit to her husband, while simultaneously the husband submits to Christ, does not mean that decisions are made in the wife's absence or without her best interest. Being the head of a family, the president of a corporation or the pastor of a church does not mean that a person makes decisions independent of counsel or chooses to delegate various responsibilities. If the man, i.e., the head of the house, feels that the wife is a better money manager, or better at disciplining the children, or at handling any other issue, then the man's role as the head of the house is to choose the most qualified person to perform a particular task. Only an insecure person obsessed with power would choose to make all the decisions without any input. The scripture previously cited in Genesis 2:18 gives us the purpose for marriage. It is not for procreation, safe sex, financial security, lust or any other secular desire. The purpose for marriage is to meet the human need for companionship. Marriage was designed to defeat loneliness.

I mentioned in the last chapter on solutions that in an African value system, the community marries you and remains to provide reconciliation. Historically, and currently in many countries in Africa, in addition to the council of elders and grandparents there was someone else to help with the reconciliation process.

I believe the best third party in marriage is the Lord. I wanted a separate chapter on this issue to explore what the Lord has to say about male/female relationships. In a previously cited scripture, we mentioned the Lord hates divorce and wants us to reconcile ourselves one to another as we reconcile ourselves to Him. Satan does not want men and women to come together because he is against family. Many of us underestimate the power of Satan. Scripture reminds us that we struggle not against flesh and blood, but against principalities. If only two people are allowed to vote, there will often be a split decision, but if the two parties are saved and have appointed Jesus Christ as Lord of their lives and of their marriage, they can always go to a third party. The Holy Spirit is always seeking reconciliation and forgiveness. Scripture reminds us that the number of times we should forgive is seven multiplied by seventy.

My wife and I laugh when we have disagreements. We both go to our respective parts of the house until one of us is encouraged by the Holy Spirit to reconcile. We still say from the secular perspective that, "I still think I'm right, but the Lord told me to reconcile." We both laugh because we know under our own volition we would not have been forgiving. It is only the love of the Lord that inspires us to be obedient. How good it is to have the Lord as the third party.

I had to accept over the years as I have studied male/female relationships that couples can break up in spite of their commitment to God and their race. I naively thought that if a couple was committed to the liberation struggle they were guaranteed to stay together. Many of these couples broke up, but individually they remain involved in the liberation struggle. The struggle itself could not keep them committed to each other. Regretfully, we just witnessed this with Nelson and Winnie Mandela.

I have also had to accept the fact that divorce affects believers. Couples in Christ, whether they are in the pulpit, the choir loft, the deacons' row, the usher board or the larger congregation, have all been touched by the ravages of divorce. The assumption that so many people on the outside of the church make is demonstrated in the statement, "I'm still a sinner trying to get my life together and when I do then I'll be ready to go to church." These individuals do not realize that the only difference between those in and out of the church is that those on the inside have confessed their sins, and they have been washed by the blood of Christ. The church is a hospital attempting to save sick souls, not a museum filled with saints!

The Lord allows us free choice and free will and is not a dictator. He says in His word that He stands at the door and He knocks but He waits for us to invite Him in. Every time that Rita and I have a disagreement, we both have free will to walk or to stay. The Lord lets us know what He wants, but the final decision is ours.

In the book titled *Husbands Who Won't Lead and Wives Who Won't Follow*, James Walker points out that often we tell people that our prayers have not been answered. In reality, prayers are always answered because communication has been established. As Pastor Jeremiah Wright preaches, the answer to petition has been delayed, but the prayer has been answered. James Walker goes further:

> And a starting point is most often our own hearts. Seldom does He change the circumstances before He changes us. When we find a battle going on in our marriage the first place we should look for a solution is where our Lord starts - our own heart.[3]

In conclusion, throughout this book we have used anecdotes and talked about how individuals say they are in love because he or she makes me feel good. We talked about people falling in and out of love, and we tried to explain the distinction between love and selflessness. If you truly love someone (i.e., Hofu Ni Kwenu - my fear is for you), you do not start and stop. There are five stages in the Greek philosophy of love which include Eros, Storge, Philos, Diakaisune and Agape. The first stage is romantic, the second is responsible behavior and the third is friendship followed by diakaisune which strives for justice and fairness. The last level, agape, is unconditional. Man's love is conditional because he feels that a person must earn it while God's love is given "in spite of," and is never earned - but by His grace. The kind of love that we need to have for and towards each other as human beings and husbands and wives is the kind of love that the Lord has for us.

This agape love that I am referring to is found in the following scripture in Isaiah:

> Israel the Lord who created you says do not be afraid I will save you. I have called you by my name you are mine. When you pass through deep waters I will be with you, your troubles will not overwhelm you. When you pass through fire you will not be burned, the hard trials that come will not hurt you for I am the Lord your God the Holy God of Israel who saves you. I will give up Egypt to set you free. I will give up Sudan and Seba. I will give up whole nations to save your life because you are precious to me and because I love you and give you honor. *Isaiah 43:1-5*

The Lord reminds us:

> For this is what I have against you. You do not love me as you did at first. *Revelation 2:4*

We can apply this scripture to our relationship with the Lord or to the romantic stage of our relationship with our mate. Many of us, when we first got saved, became involved in the liberation struggle, fell in love or changed our diet, started with tremendous zeal, desire and burning passion. Many of us from time to time in our relationship with the Lord, when a crisis arises we are on our knees, praying, reading scripture and regain the same zeal we had at the beginning. When the crisis fades and it is time to go on with our lives, often the zeal, desire and passion wanes.

Many of us thought having a good job, expensive wardrobe, luxury car, beautiful house, exotic travel and a good mate would make us happy. Little did we know that our lives would remain incomplete without a personal relationship with God. The best way to love your mate is to love God, then the Lord will teach you to love your mate in the same way God loves you--unconditionally.

At one of our church retreats, Dr. Collins made a profound statement, "As you work on your relationship with the Lord, as you become more and more like Him, as you begin to love Him the way He loves you, love begins to exude out of you. If your mate can also love the Lord the way the Lord loves you, you will find that you have God loving God. You will have God's love coming out of you and God's love coming out of your mate and oh hallelujah when you have God loving God!"

This is the agape love of selflessness within the higher divisions of the spirit that we need to strive towards. In closing, for those who still wonder about the differences between shacking, playing at marriage, or being married at City Hall versus the power of being in God's house and responding to

153

His word, I have enclosed the vows Rita and I exchanged at our wedding. I believe wedding vows should be taken seriously and should be listened to at every anniversary, and during every marital crisis.

Let's close with the Kunjufu wedding vows provided by Reverend Jeremiah A. Wright Jr:

Dearly beloved, we are gathered together here in the presence of God and before this gathering of friends, family and loved ones to join together this man and this woman in the Holy estate of matrimony - an estate that is ordained by God, blessed by Jesus through his presence at the wedding of Cana, sanctified and sealed by the Holy Spirit. Therefore, it is an estate which is never to be entered into lightly, unadvisedly nor irreverently by any.But one rather, that is to be entered into reverently, advisedly and in the fear of God. Into this Holy estate these two persons present come at this time before the altar of God to publicly profess beneath the cross of our Lord their love one for the other and their trust in our Heavenly Father who has brought them to this moment.

Jawanza, wilt thou have this woman as thy lawfully wedded wife? To live together after God's ordinance in the holiest state of matrimony. Wilt thou love, honor, protect and keep her in sickness and in health? Wilt thou be for her a pillar of strong Black manhood, one in which she may find strength and security when times are sad and uncertain, one in which she may find peace and joy when times are blessed, and one in which she may find security as you forsake all others? Will you be hers, and hers alone, so long as you both shall live? If so, answer I will.

154

Rita, will thou have this man as thy lawful wedded husband? To live together after God's ordinance in the holiest state of matrimony. Wilt thou love, honor, protect and keep him in sickness and in health? Wilt thou offer and give only unto him the mysteries of your God-given body symbolic of the mysteries of God's beauty forever new and creative? As your soul walks beside his soul on this pilgrimage back to your God who created both of your souls will you be his and his alone so long as you both shall live? If so answer I will.

Repeat after me, you are my life, you are my love. My heart belong only to you and as our hearts are in the heart of God, with these hands, I, Rita, take thee Jawanza to be my lawfully wedded husband. To have and to hold from this day forth. For better for worse, for richer for poorer, in sickness and in health. My soul gladly joins with your soul, my spirit willing joins with your spirit, my life lovingly joins with your life and my God-given body is reverently yours, and yours alone. May our union be pleasing and satisfying to our God who has brought us together. You offer me the mystery of God's love. I accept your offer and promise to love and cherish you till death do us part.

The rings that you give and receive on this day are very special, very sacred and very symbolic. They are, however, not your marriage; you are just as much married without these as you are with them. For truly two people who become one in God's heart are really one long before we get to this moment where they stand for public recognition

*of their oneness and union. But even more
important than this day, your wedding day,
what you now give and receive are sacred and
special because of what they symbolize. For
they really symbolize something much bigger
than your marriage. I would ask the two of
you in a moment of quiet reflection, after the
reception, after your friends and family have
all left and the fellowship is over and the fun
ended, I would ask when you are alone, and
there is no one there but Jawanza, Rita and
God, if at that moment you would look at them
all you would see is just how sacred they are
because of what they symbolize. Look first not
at the outside. The scriptures remind us that
the outside takes different shapes and
forms. Humans always look at the outside,
but God looks at the heart. Look at the very
heart for in the center you will see that both
of them are made in a perfect circle. No beginning no end, no start no finish, no bends
no cracks. Again something bigger than
this day, these symbolize your God who is
without beginning or end, no start or finish.
The scriptures remind us that God is from
everlasting unto everlasting, so should these
symbolize the love you share. Not a love that
starts and stops, begins and ends, bends and
cracks but a love like the love of God that
flows in concentric circles eternally. Look
again at the rings and you will notice they
are made of a precious metal, a substance that
will not change, age nor tarnish as time goes
by, symbols of your God who is changeless.
For God is the same yesterday, today, tomorrow and forever more. The God unto whom*

*our forebearers cried on the mother conti-
nent, the God to whom they cried during slavery, the God to whom we cry and say thank
God for partial liberation. That God does not
change. These should also symbolize the love
you have for each other, not a love that
changes. Many, many things in your lives will
change. Your looks will change, your friends
will change, the seasons will change, your
years will change, your family will change
but the love you share like the God you share
should not be a love that fades and tarnishes
with time but a love like the love of God that
is changeless. Let us now bow our heads and
ask God's blessing upon these symbols. We
come to you oh God at the foot of thy cross
which symbolizes you giving us your perfect
love. We come to you at thine alter which symbolizes the sacrifice you made for us. We
come to you between these two candles that
symbolize the divine and human nature of the
perfect gift of Jesus the Christ the word becoming flesh. We come to you above this book
the Holy symbol of your abiding presence in
our midst bring to you oh God these two symbols of oneness, of union, of unity, of Jawanza
and Rita becoming one flesh. Male and female, husband and wife, and as we bring them
to you we ask you to bless them oh God as
they have given themselves, we ask you to
bless then as they are received, but most im-
portantly Lord, please bless then as they are
worn. That in the daily wearing not only reflect the love of these two but your love, that
perfect love that bears all things, believes all
things, hopes all things and endures all things
because we ask all these blessings in the name
of Jesus our Lord let all the people say Amen.*

As a pledge of our love, as a symbol of our God's love and in token of the vows between us made, with this ring I thee wed in the name of the father and of the son and of the Holy Spirit. Amen.

Heavenly father, hear us as we pray, hear at this your altar on their wedding day. Show them the path you would have them take, help them to follow thee and sin forsake. In their heart oh God this day they have come to pledge their love and unity blessed by sacred vows. Make and keep them one through all eternity. Give them strength, your strength, in sorrow want or pain help them steadfast to remain. Whenever clouds should fill their skies of blue, Lord help their love and your grace shall see them through. Father until they reach life's ebbing tide may they in perfect love and peace abide. You have promised never to leave us nor forsake us, we claim that promise in this union, in their love and life together. And when life's sun shall set one day beyond a hill, it is our prayer that they will still be hand in hand. For we ask it in the name of Jesus Christ our Lord. Let the church say Amen.

Inasmuch as Jawanza and Rita have consented to holy matrimony and have written as publicly to that fact, exchanging vows here at the altar of God, giving and receiving rings as symbols of their love and of the love of God that has brought two lives in to one life. By the authority that is vested in me as a minister of the gospel, I hereby pronounce that they are husband and wife. What God hath joined together let not man put asunder.

♥♥♥♥

158

REFERENCES

CHAPTER THREE

1) Jones, Rachel L., "Singular Situation," *The Chicago Tribune*, Sunday, December 12,1993, Section 6, p.4.

2) Straughn, R.A., *Black Woman's, Black Man's Guide to Spiritual Union*, Bronx: Oracle, 1981, pp.6-7.

3) Kunjufu, Jawanza, *Black Economics*, Chicago: African American Images, 1991, p.1.

4) Staples, Robert, *Black Masculinity*, San Francisco: Black Scholar Press, 1982, p.107.

5) Kunjufu, op. cit., p.5.

6) "Commuter Couples," *Ebony Magazine*, August 1993, p.54.

7) Karenga, Maulana, *The African American Holiday of Kwanzaa*, Los Angeles: University of Sankore, 1988, pp.35-52.

8) Kristy, Norton, *Staying in Love*, New York: Jove, 1980, p.6.

9) Staples, Robert, *The World of Black Singles*, Westport: Greenwood Press, 1981, p.31.

10) Gibran, Kahlil, *The Prophet*, New York: Knopf, 1932, pp.15-16.

11) Harley, Willard, Jr., *Marriage Insurance*, Old Tarpan, New Jersey: Revell, 1988, pp.62-64.

12) Walker, James, *Husbands Who Won't Lead and Wives Who Won't Follow*, Minneapolis: Bethany House, 1989, pp.160-161.

13) Ibid., pp. 160-161.

14) Leary, Walter, "Sex In Black America: Reality and Myth," *Ebony Magazine,* August 1993, p.130.

15) Harley, Willard, op. cit., p. 79.

16) Spears, Donald, *In Search of Good Pussy*, New Orleans: Donald Spears, 1991, pp. 114-115.

17) Walker, op. cit., pp. 40-42.

18) Sims, Claudette, *Don't Weep For Me*, Houston: Impressions, 1985, p.79.

19) Ali, Shahrazad, *The Blackman's Guide to Understanding the Blackwoman*, Philadelphia: Civilized Publications, 1989, pp.62-63.

20) Ibid., pp.1-9.

21) Owens, Wendell, "Trying to make Sense out of Little White Lies," *Chicago Defender,* March 7, 1992, p.9.

22) Landers, Ann, *Chicago Sun Times,* March 21, 1983, p.30.

23) Fuller, Neely, Jr., The United-Independent Compensatory Code System Concept, Self-published, 1969, p.A.

24) Kunjufu, op. cit., p.55.

25) Cosby, Bill, *Love and Marriage*, New York: Doubleday, 1989, pp.158-159.

26)   Kunjufu, Jawanza, *Hip-Hop vs. MAAT: A Psycho/ Social Analysis of Values*, Chicago: African American Images, 1993, p.42.

27)   Walker, op. cit., p.176.

CHAPTER FOUR

1)   U.S. Bureau of the Census, Marital Studies and Living Arrangements, Series P-20, NOS 242, 323, 349, 380, 399 and 418, 1987.

2)   U.S. Statistical Abstracts, 1992, pp.18-19.

3)   Kunjufu, Jawanza, *Countering the Conspiracy to Destroy Black Boys*, Chicago: African American Images, 1990, p.68.

4)   U.S. Statistical Abstracts, Number 104, 1992, p.76.

5)   Kunjufu, op. cit., p.17.

6)   Kunjufu, op. cit., pp.41-42.

7)   Urban League Manual on the Male Responsibility Project.

8)   Jeff, Morris F.X., Jr., "Homicide among Black Men and Women Fatal Black Attractions," Edited by Nathan and Julia Hare, *Crisis in Black Sexual Politics* San Francisco: Black Think Tank, 1989, pp.145-146.

9)   Hutchinson, Earl Ofari, *The Mugging of Black America*, Chicago: African American Images, 1990, pp.51-52,59.

10)   Ibid., p.79.

11)   Mauer, Marc, "Young Black Men and the Criminal Justice System," *Chicago Tribune*, March 4, 1990, Section 4, p.3, Sentencing Project, Washington, D.C.

12)   Kunjufu, op. cit., p.55.

13)   Wilson, Amos, *Black on Black Violence*, New York: Afrikan World Infosystems, 1990, pp.192-196.

14)   U.S. Statistical Abstracts, op. cit., p.45.

15)   Gary, Lawrence, *Black Men*, Beverly Hills: Sage, 1981, p.53.

16)   Chapman, Audrey, *Man Sharing*, New York: William Morrow, 1986, p.79.

17)   Sims, Claudette, *Don't Weep for Me*, Houston: Impressions, 1985, p.1.

18)   Hare, op. cit., p. 139.

19)   Shaw, Valerie, *Himpressions: The Black Woman's Guide to Pampering the Black Man*, Hollywood: Turn the Page Productions, 1993, p. 45.

CHAPTER FIVE

1)   Amen, Ra Un Nefer, *An Afrocentric Guide to a Spiritual Union*, Bronx: Khamit, 1992, pp.28.

2)   Staples, Robert, *The World of Black Singles*, Westport: Greenwood Press, 1981, p.31.

3)   Staples, Robert, "Beauty and the Beast: The Role of Physical Attraction in the Black Community, Edited by Nathan and Julia Hare, *Crisis in Black Sexual Politics*, San Francisco: Black Think Tank, 1989, pp. 72-73.

4)   Shaw, Valerie, *Himpressions: The Blackwoman's Guide to Pampering the Black Man,* Hollywood: Turn the Page Productions, 1993, p.45.

CHAPTER SIX

1)   Amen, Ra Un Nefer, *An Afrocentric Guide to a Spiritual Union,* Bronx: Khamit, 1992, p.28.

2)   Karenga, Maulana, *Beyond Connections: Liberation in Love and Struggle,* New Orleans: Ahidiana, 1978, p.4.

3)   Kunjufu, Jawanza, *Hip-Hop vs. MAAT: A Psycho/Social Analysis of Values,* Chicago: African American Images, 1993, pp.13-14.

4)   Hare, Nathan and Julia, *The Endangered Black Family,* San Fransisco: Black Think Tank, 1984, p.175.

5)   Pietropinto, Anthony, and Simenauer, Jacqueline, *Husbands and Wives,* New York: Berkley, 1979, p.446.

6)   Amen, op. cit., pp.23-24.

7)   Ibid., pp.24-26.

CHAPTER SEVEN

1)   Welsing, Frances, *The Isis Papers,* Chicago: Third World Press, 1991, p.262.

2)   Walker, Earnestine, *Black Relationships: Mating and Marriage,* New York: Essential Information Publications, 1992, p.105.

163

3) Staples, Robert, *The World of Black Singles,* Westport: Greenwood Press, 1981, p.31.

4) Shaw, Valerie, *Himpressions: The Blackwoman's Guide to Pampering the Black Man,* Hollywood: Turn the Page Productions, 1993, pp.81-82.

5) Ibid., pp.83-85.

6) Jones, Joy, *Between Black Women: Listening with the Third Ear,* Chicago: African American Images, 1994, pp.17-18.

7) Gibran, Kahlil, *The Prophet,* New York: Knopf, 1923, pp.29-30.

CHAPTER EIGHT

1) Barton, David, *"To Pray or Not to Pray,"* WYCA Christian Radio Broadcast, April 1992, Aledo: Wall Builder Press, 1988, pp.45-47.

2) Wade, Brenda, and Richardson, Brenda, *Love Lessons,* New York: Amistad, 1993, pp.12-13.

3) Walker, James, *Husbands Who Won't Lead and Wives Who Won't Follow,* Minneapolis: Bethany House, 1989, p.18.

Love Notes

_____

_____

_____

_____

_____

_____

_____

_____

_____

_____

_____

_____

_____

_____

_____

Love Notes

_____

_____

_____

_____

_____

_____

_____

_____

_____

_____

_____

_____

_____

_____

Love Notes

Love Notes

_____

_____

_____

_____

_____

_____

_____

_____

_____

_____

_____

_____

_____

_____

Love Notes

_____

_____

_____

_____

_____

_____

_____

_____

_____

_____

_____

_____

_____

_____

_____

Love Notes

_____

_____

_____

_____

_____

_____

_____

_____

_____

_____

_____

_____

_____

_____

Love Notes

Love Notes

_____

_____

_____

_____

_____

_____

_____

_____

_____

_____

_____

_____

_____

_____

Love Notes

Love Notes

_____

_____

_____

_____

_____

_____

_____

_____

_____

_____

_____

_____

_____

_____

_____

Love Notes

_____

_____

_____

_____

_____

_____

_____

_____

_____

_____

_____

_____

_____

_____

_____

Love Notes

Love Notes

Love Notes

_____

_____

_____

_____

_____

_____

_____

_____

_____

_____

_____

_____

_____

_____

Love Notes

Love Notes

_____

_____

_____

_____

_____

_____

_____

_____

_____

_____

_____

_____

_____

_____